The Wealth of Connection

A NEW APPROACH TO
MAKING BUSINESS PERSONAL

by Vincent Pugliese

THE WEALTH OF CONNECTION

THE WEALTH OF CONNECTION

A NEW APPROACH TO
MAKING BUSINESS PERSONAL

by Vincent Pugliese

The Wealth of Connection

Printed in the United States of America.

ISBN 979-8-9859725-0-4 (Hardcover)
ISBN 979-8-9859725-1-1 (Paperback)
ISBN 979-8-9859725-2-8 (ebook)

Cover Design and Interior Design: Anthony Casto

DEDICATION

Dad,

With one sentence, you changed the course of my life. As difficult as it was to hear, it was honest, caring and tough. Just like you.

"You have a skill, but you aren't using it correctly," you told me.

Up until the moment you said those words, I felt that I had little control over the course of my life. It's not an exaggeration that my actions, vision and success all changed for the better since you told me that. I am eternally grateful to you for speaking the truth at the exact moment it was needed.

Your leadership has led to me writing this book, which I hope to impact lives by following your lead of being honest, caring, and tough.

THE WEALTH OF CONNECTION

TABLE OF CONTENTS

INTRODUCTION

Doing It Wrong Right From the Start

"Don't follow where the path may lead. Go instead where there is no path and leave a trail."

—RALPH WALDO EMERSON

As a teenager, Guns N' Roses was my favorite band. No other group brought the fury, rage, and energy I felt as a frustrated teen. Technically, they weren't a great band. Playing live, they were often sloppy. But they were the perfect band at the perfect time. Because of their reckless nature, Guns N' Roses were considered so disruptive that they frightened the entire industry. Their first video, "Welcome to the Jungle," was filmed, produced and published, yet MTV refused to play it. Music bigwigs threatened radio stations that they would face consequences by airing the video.

Finally, David Geffen, the owner of Geffen Records, coerced MTV to play the video. MTV agreed to play "Welcome to the Jungle" one time and one time only—on a Sunday night at 4am EST. But after the video played—at a time the executives figured nobody would be watching—the MTV switchboards blew up. I don't mean figuratively.

I mean literally. So many calls came flooding into the switchboard that the electronics exploded and melted the board.

The band immediately took off. Less than a year later, they were on tour as one of the hottest bands in the world. On August 16th, 1988, Guns N' Roses was the opening act for Aerosmith and classic rockers Deep Purple at Giants Stadium in East Rutherford, New Jersey. I was an angry sixteen-year-old at the time who was at that show. In fact, my claim to fame in high school was that I can be seen briefly in the video they filmed that day for their hit "Paradise City." I jumped off of a wall onto the stadium floor. The success of Guns N' Roses reached astronomical heights as they laid claim to being the biggest rock band in the world for the next four years.

Prior to that show, the guys from Deep Purple were asked about Guns N' Roses' unconventional style and approach. They could see from the beginning that Guns N' Roses had an attitude and approach that was against what every band did to "make it."

"They seem to be doing it all wrong right from the start," Roger Glover said with a smirk as bandmate Ian Paice howled in laughter at the irony.

In many ways, I believe that is exactly what this book is about. Without any business experience, degrees or certifications, Elizabeth and I started a business that, within a year, turned into a six-figure success that continued for more than twelve years. We shut that down for new challenges and have had similar successes in the worlds of online courses, book publishing, podcasting, membership sites, and masterminds all within the past six years. All of which we had little to no training getting started in.

I say all of that to tell you that in the world of business, we have done just about everything wrong right from the start. We did a subpar job in our website optimization, lead magnet generation, business development, search engine optimization, split testing, et al. We've done barely any promotion of anything that we sell, aside from being a guest on podcasts. Even still, that's more conversational, and I am awful at promotion. I've not been particularly good at sales. You name it, we've done it wrong. I've joked that I have no idea how we got into business, stayed in business, or have been able to replicate it in so many different industries. We've done very little of "best practices." We have shunned popular conventions and enjoyed doing things our way with a higher likelihood of failure than "guaranteed" success through "the way it's always done."

Yet there is one aspect of business where we did quite well. That was in the world of connections. Even with our muted business skills, I noticed I was being introduced as someone who "knows everyone." It surprised me when big names in these industries were excited to connect with me because they were told I was someone they needed to meet. But my impostor syndrome kicked in. Their numbers—whether through income or in followers—blew ours away. Still, I focused so much on connecting that they kept hearing my name and wanted to collaborate. There was no other reason why so many giants in an industry I was barely a part of were excited to endorse my first book.

The experts can throw around all of the strategies, certifications, and "Seven Step Methods" they want, but *The Wealth of Connection* is the framework that is not only incredibly simple, it is the foundation to true, meaningful success. Success financially, yes, but more importantly, with the people in our lives. Most experienced entrepreneurs will tell you that the key to success is built around relationships. And not coincidentally, stronger connections and relationships will grow your financial wealth.

The Wealth of Connection is written in five parts.

1 - CHARACTER

Character comes first. We have all encountered that person who oozes charisma and charm only to learn the hard way that they lack character. We can be fooled into thinking that charisma equals character, but it doesn't. So understanding character is a key foundational piece to building a wealth of connections. We are bombarded with messages about our goals, but focusing only on our goals leads to a self-involved approach to building relationships, which can lead to quick results but long-term frustration, damaged relationships and lack of trust. When we set generous goals that bring value to others, our goals get taken care of.

2 - CURIOSITY

Curiosity is a key trait in anyone who is well-connected. A lack of curiosity leads to countless missed opportunities that are never seen or discovered. Being curious, however, leads to asking better questions, insights into solving problems and making the people around you feel appreciated and understood. By leading with curiosity, we not only earn more trust from those in our lives but we gain insight into ideas, services and products that we can create. Our curiosity can open doors to help people who are struggling. When we do that, even greater trust is built. The foundation to *The Wealth of Connection* is character and curiosity. It is built around that. If either (or both) of these are lacking, success will be short-lived, if achieved at all.

3 - Connection

Character and curiosity lay the groundwork for great connections. Birds of a feather flock together, and nobody of quality likes being around someone who lacks character or curiosity. We might be charmed by them for a short time, or we may get wrapped up in the drama of someone who is self-involved, but both of those situations usually end poorly and often with resentment. When we display character and curiosity, we will attract those who have it too and repel those who don't. Users don't want to be around people who have solid boundaries, while helpful people love to help helpful people. This is the moment when the separation happens. Who will you attract, and who will you repel? The answer to this will determine your future success in business, relationships and happiness.

4 - Collaboration

Collaboration is the magic that brings character, curiosity and connection together. Collaboration should be known as the ninth Wonder of the World (after compound interest.) Collaboration is the fertilizer that allows everything you do to spread. It opens up worlds, it opens up platforms and it gets you connected to people you would never reach on your own. When we have character, curiosity, and connection, we build trust where others with those same qualities are not only willing to connect with us but also excited to share their ideas and insight. Collaboration is the ultimate multiplier, though it's nearly impossible to make any impact in that world without the first three parts.

5 - Creation

Why did I save creation for last? Because this is where almost everyone starts! They want to build a business, write a book, or start a podcast. But for most, nobody cares. Why? You guessed it. They didn't display the character to gain trust. They didn't have the curiosity for anything but what they were looking to accomplish. They didn't make solid connections that would lead to opportunities for great collaboration. So they do all of the "right" things business gurus tell them to do—built the website, created the logo, developed the brand and perfected the elevator pitch—but they were met with disappointing results and can't figure out why. The why is because they focused on their personal goals and not their relationships. When you focus on character, curiosity, connection and collaboration, whatever you create has an incredibly higher chance of success. Why? Because you will have built your Wealth of Connection.

Are you ready to build your Wealth of Connection? Then let's go!

Part 1

CHARACTER

Value Your Generous Goals More Than Your Selfish Goals

No Expectations

"If you want happiness for an hour, take a nap. If you want happiness for a day, go fishing. If you want happiness for a year, inherit a fortune. If you want happiness for a lifetime, help somebody." — CHINESE PROVERB

When my first book, *Freelance to Freedom,* was published, my wife Elizabeth and I decided to do something different. The idea of a book tour didn't sit well with me. It was my first book and I felt I hadn't earned the right for something like that. It wasn't like people were climbing over one another to get my signature. This was a grassroots effort to get a message out, and I was happy giving away copies to get people to read it. A book signing would feel like a phony public relations move to appear like I was something I wasn't.

So instead of a book tour, we created something a little more creative and appropriate: a Thank You Tour.

The idea blended what we believe our life of freedom should be about: spending time with our family on a three-month cross-country road trip doing work we love while thanking—in person—the people who helped us with this book and the message. It wasn't about selling books. It was about giving thanks to the people who made the book possible while having an amazing adventure with our family.

In addition to all the friends we got to see and give the book to throughout the United States, we were fortunate to hand the book to so many influential people that not only provided education and inspiration, but also endorsements. In Franklin, Tennessee, our family got to be there when I gave a copy to *48 Days* author Dan Miller, and on the same day signed a copy for Dave Ramsey, who was an important figure in that book. In San Diego, Pat Flynn of *Smart Passive Income* had coffee with our family for a few hours while discussing Coyote Peterson with our boys. At an event there, I got to thank John Lee Dumas of *Entrepreneurs on Fire* for his support. And in Newport Beach, California, I met up with Seth Godin to thank him and give him a book.

Godin was speaking for a big crowd that evening, as well as recording an interview for *Behind the Brand* with Bryan Elliott. I was hoping to grab a few minutes to thank him and hand Godin the thank-you cards—adorned with purple cows and linchpins—our kids made for him. As I handed him a copy, he kindly asked how the book launch went. He was incredibly generous to have given an endorsement for the book to this unknown author.

"The launch went great," I said. "I had no expectations."

"That's perfect," he responded, suddenly becoming serious. "*Never* have any expectations when releasing a book."

That was wise advice from someone who has written nineteen best-selling books. But another piece of advice he shared that night became a lightning rod to this message. During the question and answer session, I raised my hand. But before I could ask anything, a woman to my right got to the microphone first. Actually, she grabbed the mic and forcefully declared, "Me first!"

I was surprised. I then listened to her ironic question while waiting for another shot.

"Thank you for what you said earlier about being generous," she said. She then described her struggles with navigating her way through her corporate career and pursuing her entrepreneurial vision.

"I think that the answer is to be less selfish," she responded. "Is that the answer to my question?"

"I think that's the answer to every question," Seth responded. "Instead of wondering where the next tools will come from, the question is, who are you seeking to change? Every important entity makes a change. The more generous the change, the better."

My mind attempted to process that answer. The irony of her wondering if being less selfish was the answer after declaring "me first" in the quest for the microphone was hard to miss. Not more than a minute later, he called on me. I was taken aback by his next words.

"Vincent, tell us about your new book!" Godin said.

I was stunned. I did not want this to appear like I was looking for him to showcase my book. I brought it to him as a thank-you, and I did not want to take advantage of the situation.

"Thank you, but that's not why I'm here," I responded nervously.

"I know," Godin laughed while holding up my book. "*I'm just trying to get you some product placement*!"

In front of his audience, and a recorded show going out to a much larger online audience, he lived what he preached. He didn't need to do that. There was no benefit to his brand or business to give up the spotlight to some unknown who just published his first book. But he had placed the book under his chair, and when he saw my hand go up, something in him made him think to do that. He didn't ask me to pay him to hold up my book. He just did it to be generous.

And because of that generosity, I can't stop telling this story. I tell it to friends. I tell it on stage. I'm telling it to you. I tell it everywhere. I guarantee that the amount of attention I give to someone who does something like that is worth way more than any rate he could charge.

Seth demonstrated that the reason he has been so successful for so long is because he has generous goals. Goals that seek change to benefit others. Like he said, the more generous the change, the better. Yet, most of us focus on our selfish goals. Goals set to benefit us. Goals to sell more books, save and invest more money, gain more followers, and gain more influence. It's all about us. And it's why we struggle, just like the woman who declared "Me first!"

Me First

"Selfish people try to keep things but they lose people."

— HANNAH GARRISON

After saying goodbye to my friend, Don Wettrick, who attended the event with me, I had a ninety-minute drive back to Oceanside to process what I just learned. Not just that night but over the few months of the Thank You Tour. Why were all these good things happening? How was it possible that little ol' me was getting access to so many highly successful people while getting their support and advice and even getting my book promoted by one of the most successful marketers in the world?

I think it was because I did things the opposite of all the advice that I received. I wasn't looking to be a best-seller. I did virtually no promotion for the book. I didn't run ads, or post selfies with my book, or do any of the things I would have needed to do to get the word out. This is not a smart way to sell books, by the way. But I realized on that drive that this wasn't about that, and I think they noticed. As I cruised south on I-5 with the moonlight reflecting off the Pacific Ocean, I thought back to the woman at the event who grabbed the microphone and declared, "Me first!"

It startled me because, for so long, that was me. If I'm being totally honest, sometimes it still is. I was the person so desperate for validation and attention that I'd jump in front of someone else to get what I needed. I didn't worry about the effects of my actions because I needed something for myself.

"Is the answer to be less selfish?" the woman said again, this time in my head.

"I think that is the answer to every question," Godin replied once more. In my mind, his answer repeated itself over and over again during that drive.

Could this be the answer to the many problems, issues, and struggles I've had throughout my life? Is it really the answer to every question? I know it was the opinion of one man, and he said it off the cuff to a question he wasn't expecting, but the power of that statement was impossible to ignore. That night led me on a path of self-reflection that has been enlightening, painful and transformative. So, what was my conclusion to all that reflection?

That I'm selfish.

That's a difficult thing to say. Yet, it's the truth. I've battled selfishness my entire life, all the way to this early morning as I write this. My struggles in many ways have been because of an extreme focus on "me first." Well, what's wrong with that, you might ask? You have to focus on yourself if you want to succeed. You have to have goals and ambitions for your life. If you don't focus on yourself, how can you expect anyone else to?

There is truth in all of that.

But have you ever gotten everything you ever wanted and still felt empty? Have you ever achieved all those dreams you set and still felt alone? How can that possibly be? We're told to dream. We're encouraged to reach for the stars and get what is ours. We're told not to let anyone stand in the way of what we want, including the person in the way of the microphone.

But have you considered what comes *after* you get what you want?

I had to learn the hard way that I was focused on being the center of attention. I'm not talking about the "look at me" public figure needing to be seen. I'm talking about the always-thinking-about-me-and-my-needs center of attention. My problems. My goals. My challenges. My struggles. People may not have noticed outwardly, but to me, the world revolved around the axis of my brain.

Now, a person with selfish goals quite often accomplishes them if they are driven enough. And that was me. I was driven. I had goals. And damn it—nobody was going to stop me. But I never stopped to think about what life would be like once I accomplished those goals. What would happen then?

Consider the dog that chases its tail. Have you ever watched a dog do this? So. Much. Fun. So focused, so much energy, so much ambition. But have you ever watched a dog catch its tail?

It's not nearly as fun as chasing it is. It quite literally stops them in their tracks. *I was the dog who caught his tail*, and it sent me into a tailspin (pun intended). I was "successful" but empty. I learned how to get things—which was valuable, and still is. I had achieved everything I wanted to achieve to that point. Granted, we could always want more money. But excessive money wasn't my vice. Excessive need for validation and attention was. So when I caught the tail, it forced me to stop, look around, and finally think.

I went beyond my goals. I looked past the needs, the accomplishments, and the hardest part, the ego. And I asked myself a different question.

How do I want to be remembered?

How Do You Want to Be Remembered?

"The greatest gift in life is to be remembered." — KEN VENTURI

Scott Beynon forced me to ask this question of myself during his funeral. Even in death, he made an impact on my life. What's odd is that Scott wasn't a close family member, mentor, or teacher. He was our auto mechanic. His shop, Beynon's Service Center, was recommended to us by a friend not long after we moved to Pittsburgh. This friend raved about Scott as a person and a mechanic and told us that we *needed* to use him.

We had an issue with our vehicle that needed to be fixed. Why didn't I take a look, you might ask? When it comes to how a car works, my skills end after turning the key and blasting the radio. As you might have experienced, trying a new mechanic is stressful because if they want to rip you off, there's not much you can do to challenge it if you are not mechanically inclined. We dropped the car off and prepared for the financial impact.

Scott called us to come into the shop. When we arrived, he showed us where a hose had burst, causing a leak. After the explanation, he said everything else looked good. Our kids peeked around his shop as we asked what we owed for his work.

"Get out of here," he said. "All I did was replace a hose. I'm not charging you for that."

Seeing the kids' interest in the shop, Scott showed them around some of the tools and equipment. He didn't know it, but that day he created a long-term customer. *Few things are more valuable than an honest mechanic.* Once we find one, they not only have all of our business but all of our referrals as well.

For the next five years, any automobile issues went directly to Scott. Time and time again, he acted with integrity, humor, and honesty. If I showed up alone, he would ask why Elizabeth and the boys didn't come by, and then send home pretzels and mints for them from the giant container they loved. He occasionally let the kids work on little things at the shop, and he raved about how well they did.

"You know," he told them as he knelt to their level, "you have a job here whenever you're ready."

Not only did we always feel like we were in good hands with our cars, but he made us feel like we were his only customers. Over time, I felt like we truly were his favorites because even though they were often busy, it appeared like nobody else was around when we showed up.

One Saturday morning, I was upstairs working when Elizabeth rushed in. She looked shocked. I asked what was wrong.

"Scott Beynon died," she sobbed.

I couldn't believe it. I just saw him a few days earlier. He was the happy guy with the rough hands who treated us like we had known him forever. But I searched online and there it was: a funeral home announcement of his sudden death. He had a heart attack the night before and died almost instantly. After the shock, our first concern was wondering how we were going to tell the kids. That might sound silly, since he was our mechanic, but he was like family. More so in many ways because he was the family member you loved to visit.

The next evening, the five of us somberly drove to the funeral home to attend the wake. We didn't think we'd know anyone, and the kids were nervous, so we weren't sure we'd be there long. We arrived near the end of the viewing. Even though it was close to the end time, the place was packed. We couldn't believe how many people were inside. We hugged his son, Ryan, and all of the coworkers we'd gotten to know over the years. Story after story about Scott flowed out as we dealt with the grief by laughing about all things Scott.

As I looked around, I saw a lot of his family, but that's not why the place was packed. It was packed because of the way he made people feel. I kept overhearing all these stories about how Scott would go out of his way for this family or that family, how he would greet the kids, and how he would not charge for this or that. It was then that I had a strange feeling. I looked at his son and I paused. Then I said it.

"You know," I joked, "I really thought that *we* were special."

"He loved you guys," Ryan said, "but that's how he made *everyone* feel."

After we got home and got the kids in bed, I sat alone in the den. I couldn't help but think about my funeral. I didn't think about dying. Rather, I thought about who would show up. I thought about what they would say and how I would be remembered. And it shook me. By all accounts, Scott was a success in business, but nobody there talked about that. What they remembered was how generous, attentive, and personable he was. Most importantly, we remembered how he made us feel.

It's Not About You

"Life is a team sport. It's not about you." — SUE ENQUIST

Remembering Scott forced me to acknowledge that I still didn't view myself as an extremely generous person. I was mired in a purgatory of selfishness and helpfulness, but life certainly leaned more toward achieving what I wanted than helping others get what they want. This, in itself, was a giant leap from who I used to be. I managed to graduate from elite selfish status to a more partially selfish status.

Even my partial selfish mode didn't lead to a life of harm. I had a lot of achievements under my belt and seemed to be living a life others strive to attain.

Yet no matter what I achieved, I couldn't shake the feeling that nobody was going to be lining up at my funeral the way they did for Scott. I knew that his character and generosity made everyone around him feel like they were the only person that mattered. The funny thing is, I *knew* this was the answer. In *Freelance to Freedom*, I wrote a few pages about The Hour of Giving. That hour was the hour that began my transformation. It was the shift I needed to greet the day with a giving spirit as opposed to ruthlessly chasing my goals or wallowing in my own self-doubt. That hour each day got me out of my own head so I could feel my absolute best.

What was interesting was that I began to notice trends in my happiness, in my relationships, and even in our success in business. I would have periods of time where everything seemed light as a feather. Internally, I felt relationships were thriving and abundant. Business was easy. I felt like I had everything I wanted and more. Yet there were other times where I felt disconnected, lonely, and worried. *That's normal*, I told myself. *I bet everyone goes through that.*

The trend that I noticed, though, wasn't a trend. It was a direct result of my actions. Meaning, the times when I felt the worst were the days when I was focused on what I call my "selfish goals." What made it difficult was that I didn't feel like I was doing anything wrong during those times. But I continued to feel the discontent.

When I shift my mind from selfish goals to generous goals, life feels different. I feel happier and more connected, and see myself as a true benefit in people's lives. In my quiet time, I don't obsess over my life because the time is spent not thinking about myself. Those thoughts manifest themselves into ideas that help others. In turn, their lives improve and appreciation comes my way. Actually, appreciation and a whole lot more. Still, I somehow lost focus and forgot to make that shift a priority.

This isn't the be-all end-all business book that will solve all of your problems, but it can be the foundation for you to build around for the career success you have going forward. It will make the people in your life feel more acknowledged and, in turn, boost their success. It will connect them with people they never would have met without you. In essence, it will make the world around you a better place—and that's not even scratching the surface about what it will do for you.

A Standing Ovation of One

"Nobody made a greater mistake than he who did nothing because he could only do a little." — EDMOND BURKE

Frank Sinatra is one of the most influential musicians and artists of the 20th century. Throughout his career, he sold more than 150 million records worldwide.

At the age of 78, it was obvious to those around him that his career was reaching the end. His health failing and his mind fading, those closest to him wondered when he would give it up. Tom Dreesen, a friend of Sinatra's who had spent more than a dozen years as his opening act, explained that Sinatra had been like a father to him. Dreesen and all of the members of the inner circle were trying to figure out when he would retire. And although the crowds still could not get enough of him, Sinatra had many off nights. Throughout his career, he had always been sharp and on point, but that was no longer the case. These shows weren't labeled as a farewell tour, but the fans treated it as such. They knew this might be the final time they would see the legend, and even though they knew he was slipping, they still turned out in droves.

During one of these shows, Sinatra was three or four songs into the set when he forgot where he was in that particular song. The orchestra didn't see that Sinatra had stopped singing, which led to an awkward series of moments. The music kept going, but he wasn't singing. And the only thing that the 78-year-old could think to do was apologize.

"I'm sorry," he muttered. "I'm so sorry. I'm…I'm…sorry."

As the members of his inner circle watched from backstage, it was clear that this was going to be hard to recover from. That had to be the end. At that point, the orchestra noticed what was happening, and not wanting to make an abrupt stop, they slowed the music down to make a more seamless ending to the song and possibly Sinatra's historic career. And this wasn't a little show. There were 20,000 people in the audience, and as the music slowed and eventually stopped, the only sound was the sound of silence. A silence only broken by more apologies from the singer.

Dreesen, standing to the side of the stage, contemplated going out and assisting Sinatra off-stage, even encouraging him that it was okay to end it. To go home and call it a career. Sinatra stood there with tears in his eyes, helpless, knowing there was nothing he could do. And as he was about to place his microphone on the stool beside him and say good night one final time, a man seated at the back of the arena stood up and screamed out.

"It's alright, Frank. It's alright. We love you, Frank!" the man shouted from the darkness.

All by himself, this man began to applaud. The person next to him followed. Two turned into twenty. Twenty turned into a hundred, then a thousand, and before they knew it, the entire crowd was on their feet applauding. With the crowd going crazy, Sinatra returned to center stage. Dreesen figured this would be a great time for Sinatra to take a final bow. Instead, the icon grabbed the mic and prompted the orchestra to begin the next number, "Mac the Knife." Dreesen looked on in awe as Sinatra crushed that song. Every note, every nuance, each part of it he sang to perfection. It was like he was back in his prime as the crowd went wild.

And with everything back in place, before the next song started, Sinatra stopped once again. But instead of confusion, his eyes showed gratitude. He looked up to the top of the arena and pointed at the man who yelled out a few minutes earlier.

"I love you too, pal," he responded.

He finished out that night and resumed touring. Dreesen said that he didn't know who that guy in the last row was, but that man has no idea what impact he had. Because of him, Sinatra continued his career and thrilled crowds for two more years. All because one person took the initiative to stand up and applaud and support one of his idols at his lowest moment. It had such an impact that he single-handedly kept Frank Sinatra's career going.

It's fascinating to see how one unknown person can have such a dramatic impact on one of the biggest celebrities in the world. Nearly 20,000 people didn't do anything wrong. They simply sat as spectators, as most do. They were there to be entertained. But one person decided to be different. He decided to be a participant and not an observer. The courage and heart it took to stand up and yell out like that saved the career of his idol. It goes to show that it doesn't take 20,000 people to make a difference.

It just takes a standing ovation of one.

How Generosity Defines Our Character

"The most truly generous persons are those who give silently without hope of praise or reward." — CAROL RYRIE BRINK

To this day, nobody can identify the name of the man who gave Frank Sinatra that standing ovation. It's obvious he didn't stand up and clap to draw attention to himself. But that one moment of generosity created a memorable evening for 20,000 others and kept alive the career of one of the most famous entertainers in history. What's interesting is that every other person in the crowd was probably thinking the same thoughts as that man near the top of the arena. They were there because they loved Sinatra and wanted to see him succeed. They might have also been thinking, 'It's alright, Frank!" They wanted him to know he was appreciated. Yet only one person stood up, clapped, and yelled out his support.

But what would have happened if that guy didn't stand up? Moments later, Sinatra's people would have walked to the stage and led him off in what would have been an embarrassing ending to a legendary career. The crowd would have filed out quietly having witnessed the sad finale, and countless people would have not gotten the thrill of seeing their favorite entertainer perform over the next few years. And those 20,000 fans would have never realized that they themselves could have had a part in saving his career. Any one of them—if they understood the power of generous goals—could have been the one to rescue Frank Sinatra that night.

But how often do we think about being that person? How often do we break away from our goals, our tasks, our struggles, to simply think about what others need? Not for our own personal gain but for what someone else needs right now. What can get lost in this story is the fact that by being generous, that guy in the top row got what he came for and more. He didn't miss out on anything by simply being helpful. If anything, he gained a new appreciation for what one person can do to help another. Maybe even 20,000 others.

I wish we knew the name of the guy who gave Sinatra the standing ovation of one, yet it's appropriate that we don't. That an anonymous person can make a positive impact on the world is a lesson we all need to hear. It doesn't matter if you are in the last row—you can have a life-changing impact on others by the way you give.

Former New York Yankees owner, the late George Steinbrenner, said, "If you do something good for some other person and more than two people know about it, then you didn't do it for the right reason."

Steinbrenner was known in the media to be an ogre of a boss; a tyrant who ruled with an iron fist. During his time as owner, the stories swirled around Steinbrenner about his firing of managers, arguments with players, and other controversies that involved his gruff demeanor and abrasive personality. But what was rarely mentioned was the character behind his generosity. Even though he never discussed any of it publicly, there are countless stories throughout the New York and Tampa areas about how much he gave and how much he valued the importance of strong communities. What was only discussed by those who benefitted from his generosity was that, for thirty-two years, his foundation provided education for the children of New York area police officers, state police, firefighters, and Port Authority police who died in the line of duty.

When Steinbrenner died in 2010, stories of his generosity were relayed by the people he quietly helped. People came out of the woodwork to tell stories of him quietly giving fans signed memorabilia from Yankee players. Stories circulated about how he would keep players on the payroll long after their careers were over and provide new cars to aging former players he learned were not doing well financially. During their final days, he was known to visit players at the hospital and offer them emotional support. Story after story came out after his death that never saw the light of day while he lived. Despite all the scorn he received from the media and the public because of his harsh demeanor, he never mentioned all the good he was doing. It would have been understandable if he had, but he understood that kindness and charity were their own rewards. Not everyone had to know about it.

So whether you are the unknown person with the cheapest ticket in the last row of the arena, or the one who owns the entire stadium, two things are clear. One, generosity is what will define you after you are gone. And two, the ones telling the stories of our character shouldn't be us.

Battling Selfishness

"The only selfishness that's acceptable is striving for everyone else to be okay so that you can be even better." — JACINTO BENAVENTE

The most unhappy people tend to be the most selfish. Sad, but true. The reason why is that they are tangled up in themselves. Now, we all have issues, and nobody has it all figured out. And those of us who think we have it figured out are the ones most likely to get hit the hardest. Like author Andy Andrews says, "We are all either in a crisis, coming out of a crisis, or headed for a crisis."

The times in my life where I'm the unhappiest are the times when I'm tangled up in myself. When things were tight, I was fixated on where I could make more money. Even after things were no longer tight, I did the same. I was mentally consumed with how I could get more business. My thoughts centered on why others weren't relating to me or caring about what I thought. Do they realize how much it would help me if they shared what I was doing? I was so wrapped up in myself and what I wanted that I spent little time thinking about what others needed. And how could I? How can I be thoughtful, caring, or helpful when so much of my mental time was focused on myself? It actually felt counterproductive to be concerned with others because it was less time I had to figure out my own problems.

I would notice, either through conversations or online, the people I saw as successful. They would send a thoughtful, unexpected gift or make an impromptu business connection. And the people who were struggling would not—which becomes a self-fulfilling prophecy.

"But you don't understand," we might respond, "I need to get this going. I need to get the word out and get my business moving."

So we focus on ourselves and stay frustrated. Frustrated because we're not making the progress that we want, and even more so because nobody really seems to care. All of these people are doing awesome things and yet have no time or interest in helping me. I can tell you, for me, that led to resentment. Resentment because these people were doing well, and an even greater resentment because they weren't helping me do well. Couldn't they use their success, popularity, and platform to lift me up? To send me some work? To allow me to get what I need?

Are We Instinctively Selfish?

"Having trouble spotting a selfish person? It's about their schedule, their needs, their hurt feelings and their goals." — SHANNON THOMAS

English philosopher Thomas Hobbes stated that self-interest is the most fundamental human motivation. Studies have been done for centuries examining the mindset behind our battles between selfishness and selflessness. Kimmo Eriksson of Stockholm University studied whether people who prioritized self-oriented behavior wound up doing better in life. Eriksson compared many factors, including the number of biological children a person has, as well as their yearly income. What was interesting in the research was that 68% of the public surveyed believed that people who made more money were more selfish, but the studies showed that people with higher incomes and more children had more selfless attitudes. The title of the study stated, *Generosity Pays*.

Even more so, it's often been determined that our instincts also are altruistic. When we are asked to help in a pinch or without thinking long, humans tend to be more helpful. Yet, when we have more time to think, we pull back and are less generous. And when we are pushed against the wall—that is, desperate, anxious, and needy—our self-centeredness takes over. And, boy, has it taken over.

Do you ever wonder why you feel so alone in your pursuits? Have you sat there, numb and depressed while trying so hard to get ahead, get your message out or truly get people to care about what you do?

I always found it strange—even in the process of doing it myself—as to why we idolize and support attention-seeking sports figures, entertainers and celebrities while ignoring the wants and needs of people we actually know.

Could it be that we have slowly (or rapidly) descended to a point where, even though most of our basic human needs are being met, we collectively feel pushed against the wall by our own decisions, societal changes, and social media expectations? How do we consciously explain how we are thrilled to give more of our hard-earned money toward entertainers and athletes who wouldn't give us the time of day while allowing our friends' small businesses to suffer? When did we lose sight of how much we need support from one another individually?

Selfish Goals and Generous Goals

"How to make money isn't a bad question. It's just a bad first question."

— BOB BURG

It's important to define and clarify the difference between selfish goals and generous goals. We want something for ourselves. We want to make a certain amount of money. We want to live in a home we love in an area we desire, have connections that benefit us, and have a body to be proud of. Those are some of our selfish goals.

In many ways, selfish goals are awesome. They give us the drive and ambition to accomplish things. They can allow us to live a better life, even a healthier life, if those are the goals we choose. By achieving our selfish goals, it's entirely possible that we make the world around us better simply by what we accomplish.

But selfish goals can be incredibly destructive as well. The addict willing to do anything for their next hit will create devastating results on their life and the lives directly—and often indirectly—associated with their goals. The narcissist who is in it only for themselves will often succeed in achieving those selfish goals, particularly in the short term. We all know (or have been) that person who can't see beyond anything they want. Yet in our culture of achievement, this type of person is often lauded for their amazing accomplishments even though it's all about them. They have no problem using people to get what they want. They can fake authenticity to get people to go along with them. They can do a masterful job of pretending to help people when what they really care about is their own bottom line.

I want to be clear that obsessing over selfish goals will often get you exactly what you believe you want. And I'm under no illusion that only thinking about yourself will lead to failure or an awful life, but what I do know is that success without generosity eventually becomes empty. Sure, we don't see it in the beginning. We're so hungry—or desperate—that the idea of being generous doesn't register. We're too hyped on what we want to "waste our time" with such things. We question what the point is unless others can help us achieve our goals. Now, those who are focused on such selfish goals don't say that out loud, but they certainly say it through their actions.

My friend Chad Jeffers is a guitar player for Carrie Underwood. He's a great guy with a fascinating career, so I love to introduce him to others who have an outlet that can amplify his voice, their platform, and entertain their audience.

At a conference, a fellow podcaster told me that he was looking to interview musicians for the show. I mentioned Chad, and how I would be happy to make an introduction. Instead of accepting, he counteroffered.

"Can you get me Carrie Underwood?" he replied.

He missed a golden opportunity for an amazing connection because he couldn't see past his selfish goals.

But selfish goals should be secondary. Generous goals should be our primary goals.

What are generous goals? Goals built around something bigger than yourself. Goals that focus on the betterment of others as well as yourself. The more specific it is to a certain group, person, or idea, the more powerful the impact will be. The ironic part is that those who focus on generous goals are often the ones who far exceed the personal success of those who focus on selfish goals.

Do you know how often someone comes to me and only talks about what they want to accomplish? What their dreams and goals are? I already know where this is going, so I often have a little fun with it. Essentially, I ask how they are going to get there. They usually have no clue or have a delusional method about how it might work. When they realize that it takes other people to get there, they dive deeper into selfish mode in figuring out how to connect with these people so they can get what they want.

Wrong answer.

I advise that in order to make those connections—build that powerful network, as we say—they should focus on how they can help others achieve their own selfish goals and focus on how they personally can help these influential people. I can tell you right now that those stuck deep in selfish-goal mode don't go any further. I've learned in my coaching that these are people I don't care to work with for long. It's easy to see who gravitates toward selfish goals and those who understand the concept of generous goals.

When we focus on generous goals—ones that lift up those around us, solve problems that others are struggling with, and make others better, happier, and healthier—people naturally want to be part of it. They want to help our cause. They want to spread the word because generous people like supporting generous people.

So what happens when we just focus on our own wants and needs?

Nobody Cares

"You can have the greatest strategy in the world but what's the point if no one cares." — PATRICK DIXON

We all start somewhere. And in the beginning we all have a dream. You do. I do too. But guess what?

Nobody cares.

Sounds harsh? Good. Because it's an important place to start. But why doesn't anyone care? Usually, it's because they are so focused on their own goals. They are stressed out, anxious, and worried about figuring out their thing. They also have their own dreams, desires, and challenges vying for their attention—and they'll care less about you the more they're struggling to achieve their own dreams. They also might not care because they don't trust you—yet. They don't know you—yet. They don't care because they are tired of being taken advantage of by people that they don't have a relationship with. They don't care because just like nearly everyone else, they are driven by selfish goals.

I, too, have been filled with selfish goals. In my early twenties, I took my father's advice and chased my dream. The dream was to become a sports photographer and photojournalist. I wanted to travel and photograph amazing events and people where I could document history. I wanted access to that world. But I had no network. I had no connections. I had no trust. I was a waiter at a restaurant who knew nothing and nobody that mattered in that world.

It was at the very beginning when I heard that Pope John Paul II was making a trip to New York City. As a beginner, the idea of getting to photograph the pope was too big to not try. I figured that I would show up outside St. Patrick's Cathedral and get an image to improve my mediocre portfolio. The only problem was the pope was going to be in Manhattan on a Saturday when I was scheduled to work. I was a waiter at The Spare Rib, a restaurant on Long Island. I realized on Wednesday that I would have to find a way to get the day off.

"I can't, Vince," my boss said quickly. "Saturday is going to be packed."

I went home and learned more about the pope's trip. I *really* had to make this happen. I went back on Thursday and asked again, this time a bit pushier.

"I can't give you off on Saturday," he repeated. "Sorry—it's too busy of a night to not have you here."

I came back to work on Friday, and this was my last shot. If I couldn't get him to give me the day off, I would miss out on photographing the pope.

Before my shift started, I saw my boss in the middle of the dining room surrounded by customers and other members of the waitstaff. I took a deep breath, walked right up to him, and made a declaration. I was determined, and I raised my voice as I said it.

"I *need* to have tomorrow off!" I demanded.

He looked at me, annoyed. He responded, but he matched my volume and raised it.

"Why do you need to have off tomorrow?" he yelled, getting the attention of some of the customers as well as the staff. Without missing a beat, I matched his energy and raised my voice without realizing it so that everyone in the room could hear me.

"I need to go *shoot* the *pope*!" I yelled out.

I watched his face drop. His mouth swung wide open as he stared at me in horror. He moved his eyes around, surveying the room. I watched as my coworkers and the customers stared back at me with the same look. All at once, I heard silverware dropping on plates and audible gasps. I'd never heard a collective audible gasp in my life until that moment.

I stood there, confused. I almost got upset, about to ask what everyone's problem was, when it finally hit me. Frightened, I raised my hands to stop the psychological onslaught.

"No, No! I need to go *photograph* the pope! Not shoot the pope!" I yelled.

The collective gasp was followed by a sigh of relief and a delayed burst of laughter. My boss put his arm around me as we walked away while he wiped the sweat off his forehead.

"I can't deal with you today," he laughed. "Go shoot the pope."

Having gotten the day off, I traveled into New York City armed with nothing but my camera and a few rolls of film. The excitement of the moment faded rapidly when I realized that the closest I could get to the pope was across the street, buried behind layers of onlookers all hoping to capture a glimpse of the pontiff. As the noise crescendoed when the popemobile turned onto Fifth Avenue, I zoomed in to get the shot. But with the crowd of people around him, and the madness around me, all I got was an image of the popemobile—tiny in the frame—before he was whisked into St. Patrick's Cathedral.

I was dejected as I walked back to the train to return home. How did I ever think I could do this? I didn't know *anyone*.

The next day, I opened the newspaper to see a fantastic image of the pope on the front page of the New York Daily News from one of their staff photographers. I studied that image. I then looked at the image I shot. It didn't even look like the same event. That photographer was right next to the pope, capturing a timeless moment as he entered the historic church. My image was nothing but buildings, a lot of Fifth Avenue, and a swarm of people. If you look close enough and strain your eyes, you might catch a faint glimpse of the popemobile.

Even though I got what I wanted, it wasn't what I expected. I learned that if I was pushy enough, I could get my way. But getting my way didn't mean anyone cared about what I wanted or needed. I had no access or connections, and very few people actually cared about my goals.

I was focused on myself and myself alone. My goals were purely self-motivated, and I knew I'd never get anywhere on my own.

Be Careful What You Wish For

"When the Gods wish to punish us, they answer our prayers."

— OSCAR WILDE

Nearly two decades later, that dream was not only fulfilled, it was multiplied over and over. After shooting the pope, I did everything within my means (and often beyond it) to make sure that this dream of mine came true. I went from being a nobody with no skills, connections, or money to being an internationally acclaimed photographer with twenty years in my dream career. You name it, I shot it. Super Bowls, World Series, U.S. Presidents and world leaders, A-list celebrities, the most fascinating personalities both famous and obscure, and that doesn't even begin to tell the story.

I fought (sometimes literally), crawled (also literally) and clawed my way into the ideal career I envisioned in my most desperate times. The skills developed during that growth period led to me becoming a sought-after photographer who parlayed those skills into a lucrative career in the corporate and wedding photography world.

That world can make you drunk with attention. I was no celebrity, but people vied to be my assistant. They wanted to know the details of this crazy little world. They asked which celebrity was the nicest, or about the inside scoop on a certain person or if they could hang along during one of the shoots. It was intoxicating at times and a true ego booster, something this insecure kid from Long Island craved. But a nagging feeling hung over me after the years dimmed my excitement.

Why was I doing this? Why was I in this line of work? That was a difficult question to answer. I had to dig down and do an audit of myself and my career and answer that question.

That question led to another question that was even harder for me to answer but was at the root of what was bothering me: whom was I helping?

In the wedding world, we were providing valuable images for a family's special day, but we felt increasingly like a cog in a bloated industry built around excess. In the corporate world, I had a harder time drawing any inspiration beyond it paying well. In the sports and journalism worlds—the reason I did photography in the first place—the audit returned the verdict. I did it for me. I was inspired only by selfish goals. It was all about the portfolio I'd create, the stories I'd be a part of, and the access I would get. Me, me, me.

Nobody tells you this in school, but when you chase selfish goals and then attain them, emptiness follows. An emptiness that is hard to explain. And you never see the pain coming because you are too wrapped up in yourself to understand. Much like that time I went to shoot the pope, I realized nobody cared. Well, not entirely. They wanted to hear the stories and meet cool people. But if I died that day, nobody was coming to my funeral and talking about me the way they talked about Scott Beynon. And that haunted me.

Why did this bother me so much? Why couldn't I leave well enough alone? There was no reason to rock the boat. With a growing young family, we were in great shape financially and time wise. Yet I felt this need to burn it all down and start over.

The moment hit unceremoniously inside a dimly lit side room at the Allegheny Country Club during a wedding reception I was photographing. Weddings paid very well. It was never a passion of mine to photograph weddings, but it allowed us to transition out of the downward spiraling newspaper industry to a more secure financial career, one which freed up a boatload of time. Like many other entrepreneurs—and this is particularly true of employees—the lure of money created my passion for the work. It's easy to get blinded by the numbers when the numbers look good.

I sat down for dinner next to the DJ with a few other vendors around us. We had worked with this DJ many times as he was highly respected. It didn't take long for him to open up about his situation, and like us, things weren't going as he hoped. Business was struggling, and he didn't know how to change it. I had no training in this, and I wasn't a "coach," but I could have these conversations all day long. To brainstorm problems and come up with unexpected solutions for someone who needs help in their career and business lit a fire under me. Any chance I could, I got lost in those conversations.

Somewhere between the salmon and the strawberry cheesecake, the lightbulb went off in his head. Something I said clicked, and he saw his perspective tilt. A smile appeared, followed by a look of promise. He shook my shoulder, stood up straight, and gave me a huge thank you. He told me he had to get the music ready for the first dance, but he wished we could talk longer. I sat there and wished we could talk longer too. In fact, I looked toward the ballroom and wondered what I was doing there. I didn't want to be a vendor. But that's what I was. I was the one who took the pictures, but the value I love to bring to others through conversation and connection was missing. How did this go wrong? Sometimes, you can spend too long getting good at the wrong things.

How could it be that I was more excited to talk to someone for free than to get paid really well for being a vendor?

"If I can help people like him with their businesses while having conversations like that for a living..." I said to myself.

It was the first time in a long time that my goals weren't just about me. Yes, I wanted to shoot great images for our clients, but the motivation was a better portfolio so we could get better and higher-paying clients. I could pretend otherwise, but it was true. This felt like the opposite. I was sure I could get paid for doing this coaching thing, but money wasn't my motivation. I really wanted to help this guy out.

Achieving your selfish goals fuels you, but they only get you so far. Finding and refining your generous goals will take you—and those around you—to the top.

Do What You Want (For Others)

"In about the same degree as you are helpful you will be happy."

— KARL REILAND

What is it that you want?

I can tell you what I want. I want personal connections and real friendships. I want people to read this book and enhance their lives. I want them to see that by being more generously connected, they make those around them better while making themselves feel better. To do all that, this needs to be a great book, so I'm spending more time writing this than you might imagine. The fact that it's important to me makes it worth the time, even if there's no guarantee it will have any success. To have that opportunity, I want people to talk about the book—and that will only happen if I write a great book. To make that happen, I want people to share the book and leave reviews. I want to get on podcasts to talk about the book.

I write that as therapy because people often ask how they can help, which is good because I always struggle asking for help. I write it here as a cop out. I'm openly letting people know that I need help. That I want help.

So what is it that you want? Do you know? Do others know? It's important to let those who celebrate you know how they can help. At the same time, the reason why you might not be getting that help is because you don't have enough people celebrating you. If you don't have people celebrating you, it's hard to actually get what you want. But a reason why you aren't being celebrated might be because you aren't celebrating others enough.

I have learned that I can't worry about what I want if I'm not doing for others what I want for myself. I want people to reach out and care about me as a person. Am I doing that for others first? I want people to leave reviews for my work, but am I leaving reviews for others who have helped me? I want to get on podcasts to talk about the book's content, but am I connecting others so they get on podcasts? I want people to invest in themselves because there is no better investment that they can make for themselves. Yet, am I investing in myself?

What we want for ourselves, we need to do for others first.

Is Generosity About Money?

"Money is but one venue for generosity. Kindness is an even more valuable currency." — ALAN COHEN

Most people associate generosity with money. They think of donations and charities. We're trained to think that if we give 10% of our income to our church or send a check to an organization during the holidays, we are being generous. But often being generous has little to do with how much money we donate. Generosity has more to do with character. Some of the most awful humans I've met in this world donate tremendous amounts of money.

Generosity is the time and attention we give to other people. Generosity is the curiosity we have for someone else. Generosity is leaving a great review for the restaurant that just gave you a wonderful experience. Generosity is sharing your honest voice. Generosity is telling the hard truth to a friend when nobody else has the courage to. Generosity is creating a product so valuable that it changes the lives of others. Generosity is reaching out to a friend you haven't talked to in years just to see how they are doing.

Generosity is giving to others.

We can be generous with our time, our energy, our network, our praise, our challenges, and our words. Quite often, being generous has a much greater positive impact than a financial donation. But we have been persuaded into believing that monetary gifts are the most valuable. It explains why writing that check for a charity as a yearly tax deduction seems like the right thing to do but doesn't elicit the same emotional feeling as personally seeing and feeling the impact of your generosity.

But we have so much more to give than money. Besides, what happens to people who have money? Are they no longer eligible for receiving in life? And what about the people who don't have much money to give? Are they any less valuable due to their lack of funds?

When we realize the value we can bring to others, it opens up our world in terms of confidence, connections, and value.

Everyone can help anyone, and no matter how successful you think a person is, every person needs help with something.

Helper's High

"Thousands of candles can be lighted from a single candle, and the life of the candle will not be shortened. Happiness never decreases by being shared.."

— BUDDHA

We have all heard how social media is engineered to manipulate our emotions to keep us addicted to our phones, apps, and video games. Those constant notifications are created so that we are constantly looking at our phones and engaging others online. Judging by how fixated we are on our devices, I'd say they have been remarkably successful. One of the reasons why it is so addictive is because every time you get one of those notifications—the red announcement, the ding, the buzz—it releases a chemical in your body called dopamine.

Dopamine is produced in our brains, and when released, it creates a positive feeling in our minds. The problem is that not everything that creates this release is from something positive. The creators of social media apps know and exploit this, engineering them in ways that give us that hit of dopamine every time we receive a notification. So, with each notification, the cycle continues and the addiction builds. Given the sheer amount of time that we spend online, there is an endless supply of dopamine hits ready to go, sending our society into a spiral of addiction, bringing with it the consequences of depression, anxiety, poor sleep, and worse.

So how do we combat such a formidable adversary?

Did you know that our brain also releases feel-good endorphins each time we do an act of kindness? This was created to motivate us to do good things. This has been called the Helper's High. What is fascinating is that it doesn't just affect us in the short term. It has also been proven to help us live longer. Endorphins are a group of opiate proteins which affect our brains like morphine. These pain-relieving endorphins occur in the brain's pleasure centers. When our body releases endorphins, oxytocin, dopamine, and serotonin, it boosts our mood while blocking our stress hormone (cortisol). It's obvious to see how giving makes us happier inside and wards off stress.

Studies show that people who are the most generous receive the Helper's High because they have higher levels of oxytocin, the biochemical most associated with social bonding and love.

Is Generosity Good for Your Health?

"The meaning of life is to find your purpose.The purpose of life is to give it away." — PABLO PICASSO

There are so many ways in which generosity benefits the people around you and makes all the connections in your network stronger. But what most don't know or have forgotten is that it bounces back to you because high-quality people want to be around generous people. Of course, there is another area where generosity will help you.

Your health.

A ten-year study conducted at the University of Michigan tracing more than 2,700 people found that men who did regular volunteer work had death rates 2.5 times lower than men who did not volunteer regularly. People who are self-involved are often thought of as being egotistical, but that ego often derives from pain: the pain of abandonment, the pain of loss, or the pain of being alone. Often, those who suffer those types of pain shield themselves from further pain by getting wrapped up in themselves.

They unintentionally become self-centered, often leading to deeper depression. It gets harder to think of others when you get into your own head like that. Fortunately, generosity distracts us from those feelings and any negative self-talk. It seems counterintuitive, but active generosity actually repels feelings of depression and isolation. It turns out that when we care for others, we care more about ourselves.

Also, being generous has been proven to lower cholesterol, inflammation, blood pressure, stress levels, depression, and anxiety. It has further been shown to improve our self-image and make us more empathetic, because we are forced to think outside ourselves. According to psychologist Chloe Carmichael, building these relationships "strengthens our sense of community and safety because we are more likely to get support in the future from people we are helping today."

Did you catch that? We are more likely to get support in the future from the people we help today. So many of us—me included—had it wrong for so long. The ironic part is that your goals will be achieved and expanded upon, and much faster, by focusing on other people's wants and needs.

Forced Generosity

"Forcing people to be generous isn't humanitarian, effective, compassionate or moral. Only acts that are truly voluntary for all concerned can be truly compassionate." — HARRY BROWNE

Generosity does not mean being a doormat for the selfish. As many advantages as the generous possess in life, one of the disadvantages is becoming prey for the self-centered. The euphoric feel of generosity can be smoked out by what I call the "parasites." By nature, parasites live on or inside of something, and they get their food from the host. When they get their fill, they leave for the next victim. These two types of people have diametrically opposed mindsets.

Parasites are not only driven, they are cunning. Oftentimes they don't intend to be self-centered, but their upbringing, insecurity, or lack of confidence leads them to constantly look for what they can get. And when you match up someone looking to give with someone looking to get, it results in a lopsided relationship. These energy suckers are masters at knowing who will be an unsuspecting victim of their mental warfare. These people know that the generous with boundaries will not stand for their manipulation. They learn quickly that they won't get what they want and move on.

Yet, when they find that generous soul with a great heart—often known as people pleasers—they know they have found their match. Needy and often charismatic, the parasites initially satisfy both parties. The people-pleaser feels special because they get to help a needy soul. They might spend hours in conversation offering support and solving their friend's problems. In the early stages, they don't see that the majority of the conversation is all about their friend and rarely, if ever, about them. When it is, after lip service, the parasite often uses their charm and neediness to quickly bring the conversation back to them.

It could be weeks, years, or a lifetime before the people pleasers identify the parasites. Unfortunately, this isn't uncommon inside of families. The parasites use guilt and emotional manipulation to get what they want. Whether it's for a family member to stay close by, support a family member financially, or be an emotional punching bag, these slick manipulators know how to pull the levers—and they aren't afraid to use them.

So what happens when the people pleaser notices that this person is a parasite intentionally sucking the life out of them? They naturally pull back. The people pleaser feels used, betrayed, and confused. They want to believe that this is a real friendship based on mutual care and respect, but would a person who cares and respects you intentionally take from you to their benefit and not yours?

They use their guilt to force generosity. Their strategy is built around the idea that they are the victim and the people pleaser is actually selfish for not helping them. The parasite has done such a masterful job of crafting this narrative that the people pleaser becomes confused, afraid that if they don't do what is asked, they will feel shame for not being a good friend. They are fearful of losing that friendship altogether.

This is *forced generosity*. Nothing about this type of giving is generous. This is enabling. By giving (and giving in), the people pleaser is actually doing harm to their "friend" and their relationships. They are, in essence, giving a drunk a drink. They are allowing this person to enhance their ability to manipulate others. By going along with it, they themselves begin to lose faith in the specialness they possess in their heart for caring for other people.

"Shouldn't we love everyone?" some might ask. "Shouldn't we try to help everyone?"

Absolutely. But love and help isn't always given in the way everyone wants it. Love and help, in this case, is more effective by not allowing someone to take advantage of others.

Saying no to manipulation is a generous act.

Charisma Is Not Character

It's true that charisma can make a person stand out for a moment, but character sets a person apart for a lifetime." — JOHN C. MAXWELL

Don't confuse charisma with character. Just because they are two completely different things does not mean they are mutually exclusive. Many of us had to learn the hard way that they are not the same. Charisma is something that attracts people. We've all met those charismatic people who can draw others to them. Their charm can seduce very easily.

Adam Grant, in his book *Give and Take*, gives the example of Enron CEO Ken Lay. Enron was an oil and commodities firm in the late 1990s and early 2000s. Lay had tons of charisma and was able to build an outstanding network around him. But there is a danger in building a network if you don't do it the right way. He built a network to gain influence and get those influencers to do what he needed them to do. He catered to them, but he didn't care about the people he was serving. Lay strategically targeted people like President George H.W. Bush and his circle. He eventually got close to them. From there, he used that connection to get close to Bill Clinton. Lay used those relationships to leverage to his advantage and influenced regulations that benefitted his company.

This could have been long-term powerful networking if it was done with integrity and character. Behind the scenes, though, was a different story. Wall Street came in to evaluate Enron, and Lay had seventy employees pretend to be doing jobs they weren't doing to make it seem like the company was more valuable than it was. He exploited his employees to get what he wanted. Once investors and others found out Enron was a train heading off of the tracks, Lay sold seventy million dollars' worth of shares right before Enron collapsed. The business was investigated, destroyed, and every one of those people lost their jobs. Lay died of a heart attack shortly thereafter.

Lay was a person who had a lot of charisma, was extremely charming and able to win people over, but that did not equate to character. The key is to not be fooled by one while thinking it's the other. And highly charismatic people can often fool others. Lay was able to fool some of the most influential people in the world with his charisma. And the charisma shielded the fact that he wasn't concerned about making his employees' or new friends' lives better. His intentions were to take advantage of their influence and connections to get what he wanted. This can happen to any of us if we don't pay attention to the people surrounding us. There are a lot of people walking around oozing charisma and bravado without character behind it.

Don't confuse charisma with character.

Be Generous with Your Honesty

"Being honest might not get you many friends, but it'll get you the right ones."

— JOHN LENNON

One of the musicians that I heard played at home when I was a kid was Billy Joel. Being a fellow Long Islander, there was a pride in having a hometown person make it to superstardom. His *52nd Street* album was one of the first I remember carefully placing the needle onto the vinyl in our small living room. On that album was a song titled "Honesty." That might have been the first song in my life where I deeply felt the lyrics.

It struck me, even at ten years old, how rare honesty was. I was confused by how someone could be so nice to a friend and then tear them down when they walked away. I was consistently disappointed when someone gave a soft, gentle affirmation of someone else's work, only to later tell others how awful the work was.

My curious brain asked why they would intentionally say

something they didn't believe to someone they were friends with. The answers were interesting. They didn't want to hurt anyone's feelings. They didn't want to get into an argument. They hate confrontation. They didn't think the person could handle the truth or would value their opinion. And one of the most curious of all: they didn't want to damage their friendship.

This might explain why I had trouble keeping friends. Even now, I can't understand how much value can come from a friendship where you can't tell the truth. Intrinsically, it's the foundation for a shallow, surface-level relationship. I mean, you have someone who does not truly want the truth even though they ask for it. The online version is the business owner/author/podcaster who asks only for five-star reviews. What if your content isn't five-star worthy? Are you interested in honest feedback, or are you looking to have only favorable reviews for your benefit? What if your content isn't good? Do you not want to improve?

If someone can't handle the truth, their friendships will always be shallow. Even worse, they will become delusional due to their need for constant positive praise and attention. Few people will feel comfortable giving honest feedback because they will fear the reaction. So this person actually gets an inflated opinion of themselves. No honest feedback gets in, no improvements seem necessary, and they will be crushed or slip into denial when they are finally faced with the truth.

On the other hand, the person not willing to risk the friendship by sharing the truth is also at fault. Is that person so in need of a friend that they can't risk losing one by saying what they believe? Are they so afraid of rejection that they would rather be friends with someone who doesn't value honesty?

Being honest is generous. If done in a tactful, caring way, it can be the greatest gift we ever receive. Joe Elbert was one of the top photo editors in the nation but brutally honest. While in college, I had an opportunity to get a portfolio critique from him. Half of our class refused to bring their portfolio to Elbert because they were afraid of what he would say. They had portfolios they had worked on, in some cases, for years. And they didn't take the opportunity to be critiqued by the best because they were afraid of the truth.

I decided to not run from the truth. So I waited in line for my beating. It didn't make it easier that the guy in front of me got torn apart by Elbert. He succinctly and meticulously pointed out the flaws in his execution, positioning, and vision. He gave blunt and valuable suggestions on what he could do to improve. He didn't pull punches. I wouldn't be honest if I said I didn't think about walking away and avoiding my beating. I watched that guy walk away with his head down as I took a deep breath and stepped forward.

I handed him my sheet of twenty slides—my absolute best work. I might as well have been naked in that ballroom because I felt completely exposed and vulnerable. He quietly studied all twenty images. Without the fire that he brought down on the last kid, he matter-of-factly pulled out two slides and pushed them toward me. I felt good. I told myself that I'm doing well. He only eliminated two images. For the first time, he looked up and looked me in the eye.

"There is your portfolio right there," he stated, pointing at those two images. "Get rid of the rest. Those two images have everything you need and will live on. That is your new portfolio."

I was crushed. There were eighteen images in there that I had sweated over and bled to get. Endless hours of travel, work, and struggle to get them. My best work rejected. I walked away toward the closest couch with my heart in my stomach. Yet at the end of that walk I had a pivotal shift. I said to myself, "If I ever want to get to the highest levels, those eighteen images aren't going to get me there. These two images will."

I pulled out an empty slide sheet and put those two images in. I discarded the other eighteen into my backpack.

As deflating as it felt, I said to myself that I have two. I now have a standard that all future images need to live up to. That got me to raise my standards and push me to a higher level that, within one year, allowed me to win the William Randolph Hearst National

Championship as the top college photojournalist in the nation. That never would have happened if he wasn't generous with his honesty.

If he would have done what just about everyone else does—which is to say, "These look great"—I would have never launched the rocket ship of a career I did over the next decade. It's easy to say what people want to hear, but if you actually care, be the kind of friend willing to risk a friendship by being generous with your honesty.

Create Your Own Thank You Tour

"Feeling gratitude and not expressing it is like wrapping a present and not giving it." — WILLIAM ARTHUR WARD

I didn't know who John Kralik was when we created the Thank You Tour that went with the launch of *Freelance to Freedom*. I had never heard of anyone doing that before, which is a part of why it was so appealing. I truly believe the success of the book and everything that came afterward came more from the relationships created, developed, and strengthened through that tour than any other form of marketing or promotion. Little did I know that seven years earlier John published a book titled *365 Thank Yous*.

John was where so many people struggling in life find themselves. Constantly focused on what he didn't have, he was failing in all areas of his life. At fifty-three years old, his law firm was on the cusp of going out of business. Not only was he at the end of a second painful divorce, he had terrible relationships with his two oldest children. John became yet another person down in the dumps who felt like life was handing them one problem after another. To pile on, his newest girlfriend had just broken up with him, his tiny apartment was blazing hot in the summer/ice cold in the winter, and various health problems had him feeling as low as possible.

On New Year's Day, John went for a hike to get his mind off of his pain and focus on his gratefulness. Days earlier, he sent a Christmas gift to his ex-girlfriend. She sent back a simple, handwritten note that got him thinking. That note reminded him of his grandfather, who always sent a thank-you note along with a silver dollar.

To shift his mindset, he took on a challenge. He, too, would write thank-you notes. After focusing for so long on his problems, John wanted to turn the tide and make other people feel special. He had one stipulation: he would not do it electronically because those messages are often and easily forgotten. So he sent out a handwritten thank-you note every day for a full year.

The notes started with thank-yous to his children. With a daily goal, he continued to send notes to his old friends, his landlord, ex-spouses, and even a helpful barista at Starbucks. But it didn't take nearly a year for his note-writing to have an impact. Not only were the notes appreciated by people with whom he had challenging relationships, but unexpected goodness began flowing into his life. Without asking for it, he got repaid for past generosity. For someone used to blaming everyone else for his terrible life, he couldn't help but notice how different those people were when shown gratitude rather than expectation.

What was eye-opening for John was that the people in his life were no different than they were before. He just treated *them* differently. He continued past the 365 days of note-writing all the way through for 15 months and watched frigid friendships become warm again and good ones turn into truly great relationships.

"Through the process of writing thank-you notes," John wrote, "I had developed a notion of being blessed with grace that was meaningful to me. And I could see this grace and these blessings everywhere—in my sons, daughter, siblings, friends, and colleagues, for just a few of more than a hundred examples—where I had not seen it before."

John's story is one of gratitude and redemption, yet it reveals that what so many crave is appreciation. Being appreciated goes to a core feeling in life: feeling valued as a human. When we feel appreciated, we inherently feel liked, noticed, and connected.

Could it be that happiness and success means less goal setting and more thank-you tours?

The Value of Character

Character is foundational. If your character is already generous rather than selfish, you have the first piece to build upon. All of the other things we discuss in *The Wealth of Connection*—Curiosity, Connection, Collaboration, and Creation—will be diluted, damaged or destroyed without a character of generosity. We will miss opportunities we never see and damage things we currently have.

The selfish only do well in the short term. It's easy to say what you need to say in order to get what you need to get at the moment. It takes character to be generous with your honesty. It takes character to write thank-you notes to those who have helped you while not expecting anything in return.

Being selfish is normal. But do you really want to be normal? Do you see that the "Me First" approach brings little goodwill? Does it make sense that having no expectations is a fantastic way to approach relationships? Easy to say but hard to do. You can hustle, work hard, and set goals only to find out no one cares about your needs without having a real relationship.

Things didn't prosper—at least they didn't for me and I suspect many of you—until I realized it wasn't all about me. When we do what we want for ourselves for others, we feel that Helpers High. We see how generosity is good for our health and our character. We also know that charisma is not character and why we shouldn't force generosity.

Generosity, it turns out, is the foundation of character.

Part 2

CURIOSITY

Value Questions More Than Answers

What an Encounter with the Mafia Taught Me About Curiosity

"If knowledge is power, then curiosity is the muscle."

— DANIELLE LAPORTE

When I was fifteen years old, I hated school but loved the New York Mets.

I studied their roster and stats much more than I studied math and science. The Mets, after years of struggle, had won the World Series six months earlier. I watched nearly every one of their games that season. I tried to leave school to go to the victory parade in Manhattan, but my mom wouldn't let me.

April 7th, though, was opening day for the world champion Mets—the day they would raise the banner and receive their championship rings. I had to be there. After weeks of badgering, I convinced my parents to let me go—and they agreed under one condition. My friend, Scott, had to go with me. After convincing Scott to go, we were set. My parents left for work, and I walked over to his house. It was then he told me his mother changed her mind. He was no longer allowed to go.

I walked back to my house unsure what to do. I had heard the phrase that it's better to ask forgiveness than permission, but I had never had the chance to use it.

Until then. So I walked to the bus stop, which would take me to a second bus, and finally to the 7 train, which would get me to Shea Stadium. The first bus ride was uneventful, and the second appeared the same as I got on. It was just me, the bus driver, and a really large man dressed all in black sitting next to the driver laughing and telling stories. I was intimidated as I intentionally walked to the back of the bus. A few minutes into the ride, I heard a question hurled in my direction from the front of the bus.

"Hey, kid, shouldn't you be in school?" the voice shouted.

"I'm, uh, going to the Mets game," I resounded meekly.

"By yourself? Do you have a ticket?" he asked loudly.

"No, I'm going to try to get one at Shea," I quietly said.

He responded quickly, "Kid, this game's been sold out for months. It's the hottest ticket in town. How much money do you have?"

"I've got thirty dollars," was my proud but pathetic answer. He smiled while shaking his head.

I put my head down to avoid any more questions. I suddenly realized that I might not have a clue about what was ahead of me. I avoided the conversation until we got to my stop. I walked past the man, getting out as fast as I could. As I got to the bottom step, I heard his voice one final time.

"Hey, kid," he repeated, only a little softer that time. "Now listen to me very closely."

He had my full attention.

"When you get to Shea," he said, "go to Gate B. Ask for Vito. Tell him Funzi from the Waterfront sent you. You got it?"

"I got it," I responded.

"Now go," he demanded.

I was bewildered. Should I trust him? What was he doing? Why did he tell me that? I got on the 7 train still planning on scalping a ticket. But I kept repeating those three things: Vito. Funzi. Gate B. Vito. Funzi. Gate B.

When I got to Shea, I was overwhelmed. It was wall-to-wall Mets fans dressed in blue and orange. Half of them were looking for tickets. Nobody was selling. And if they were, $30 wasn't going to cut it. Funzi knew what he was talking about. Plan A wasn't going to work. I had to go to plan B, which meant going to Gate B. I walked up to the usher at Gate B, where there were only a few people, most of whom already had passes.

"What do you want?" the old man working the gate snapped.

"Uh…is, um…Vito here?"

His head lifted as he looked into my eyes.

"Funzi sent me," I said, pointing behind me at nobody in particular. I looked down at his hands and watched him unlock the silver gates.

"Come on in," he said swiftly. Just like that, I was on the other side. It's like I was given the secret code. Funzi and Vito were the secret code!

"Wait here," he said as he got on the radio.

Less than two minutes later, a young lady with dark hair and a big smile greeted me.

"Follow me," she said kindly as we walked up the ramp into the crowded stadium.

"Are you hungry?" she asked.

"Uh, sure?" I responded.

She took me to the concession stand and got me a hot dog, soda, and Cracker Jacks.

"Would you like a program?" she asked.

"Um, sure?" I mumbled again.

She got me a program. Before I knew it, we were in the concourse headed through the short dark tunnel where all I could see was the beautiful green grass of the baseball field of my favorite team. As we got closer, I started to wonder if it was really happening. After we emerged from the tunnel, right behind home plate overlooking the field, I knew what was happening: the World Series celebration was about to begin.

The banner was raised high into the air, and I was so close I could see the diamonds shining on the Mets World Series rings. After Darryl Strawberry crushed a three-run homer in the first inning, I thought I had died and gone to heaven. The excitement inside the stadium was something I hadn't experienced before, and I quickly remembered that I "should" be in science class at that moment.

The Mets defeated the Pirates, 3-2 and I was the happiest kid in the world.

Curiosity Did What to the Cat?

"Judge a man by his questions, not his answers." — VOLTAIRE

Funzi gave me one of the most memorable experiences of my childhood by using a combination of the pillars of *The Wealth of Connection*. The one I want to focus on here is Curiosity.

It's interesting how curiosity is seen in our culture. Come to think of it, what is the first phrase that comes to mind when you think of curiosity? If I am reading your mind, well, you just thought about how curiosity killed the cat. Now think about that. Curiosity *killed* the cat. It doesn't say that curiosity gave the cat more insight into what was going on around it. It says it *killed* it.

We've been trained to be heard rather than learn. I love to talk, but I don't learn by talking. Learning is done by listening to others, what their struggles are, and what their dreams are.

Funzi was curious. He asked questions. Actually, he didn't talk about himself at all. With only three questions, he was able to learn enough about me to do something that gave me the experience of a lifetime. So many of us try to give advice before we know the situation. Funzi didn't give any advice or guidance *until* he asked enough questions.

It's clear that we don't ask enough questions. And even if we stop ourselves from talking about ourselves, we aren't asking enough *meaningful* questions.

Most people want to talk about themselves. It's inherent in all of us. The sweetest sound to a person's ears is the sound of their own name. Yet asking questions allows others to feel good about themselves. The greatest thing people want is to feel appreciated. It's a gift when you ask about them because so few people actually do.

What if Funzi talked about himself? What if he talked about his life? Well, actually…I wish he would have. I am quite curious about him. But let's examine what he did. After initiating the conversations and being bold, he started asking questions.

"Shouldn't you be in school?"

My answer gave him some valuable information. I'm sure when I told him I was going to the game, he got curious.

"Do you even have a ticket?"

If I answered yes, the conversation would have gone in a different direction, or possibly ended. But I told him no. That must have gotten him a bit more curious. I can only imagine he knew how tough a ticket was to get even if I'd be able to afford it. I'd also guess that this was the point he started thinking about Vito.

His next question gave him all the information he needed.

"How much money do you have?"

When I told him that I had thirty dollars, knowing what I know now, Funzi knew what he was going to do. *I want you to understand that the person who asks the questions controls the conversation.* All of the growth—and all of the accomplishments—I've gotten in my life have come from asking questions. Asking questions shows that you have a beginner's mindset. That mindset shows you are always looking to learn.

But why are we so hesitant to ask questions? Is it because we are so self-absorbed that we don't care? Yes. Many of us are. One of the reasons why is that we've been trained to be less curious.

Are We Trained to Be Less Curious?

"A sense of curiosity is nature's original school of education."

— SMILEY BLANTON

Any parent can tell you how curious children are. It's been said that kids under five ask an average of a little over one hundred questions per hour! Yet Susan Engel, the author of *The Hungry Mind,* discovered something troubling. Through her team's research, they discovered that once kids reached school age, they asked between two and five questions per hour. By fifth grade, there were stretches where the kids didn't ask a single question.

So what happened to their curiosity? Did they naturally lose it? Or was it sucked out of them by a system that doesn't value curiosity? With such an emphasis on grades, tests, and compliance, curiosity is actually a detriment to the mission of the modern school system.

Imagine that six-year-old sitting in class amazed by the world around her. So many things fascinate her, including the birds outside. As her teacher discusses the current subject, this little girl notices the most interesting bird through the window. What kind of bird is that? What makes it so colorful? What does it eat? Dozens of questions run through her curious mind all at once.

Excited, she points out the bird to her teacher. The teacher has a lesson to teach so he shuts the girl down politely and tells her to pay attention to the lesson. The girl tries, but she's much more interested in the bird than whatever lesson is being taught. So she is forced to ignore what she is curious about and pay attention to something she isn't interested in. This is right about the moment where we begin training our kids to be less curious. After six years of rapid learning through curiosity, they are now being told to stop asking questions. And it continues at such a quick pace that by the age of ten, they don't even bother asking questions anymore.

So we wind up with "high-performing students" looking to get better results on tests and being less curious while we know that the curious have a deeper understanding of and interest in the topics they study. Once this is understood, we start to understand how those who have achieved the awards, the grades and the high-profile degrees struggle once they get out of the bubble of academia.

Grades don't create champions. Curiosity does.

The Champions of Curiosity

"Communication—the human connection—is key to personal and career success."— PAUL J MEYER

Tom Brady is widely regarded as the greatest NFL quarterback of all time. In eighteen years as the primary starting quarterback for the New England Patriots, he led them to seventeen division championships, thirteen AFC Championship Games, nine Super Bowl appearances, and six Super Bowl championships. At the age of forty-three, after failing to get an offer from the Patriots, he signed with the Tampa Bay Buccaneers who had a losing record the previous season. With no offseason or training camp because of Covid-19 and with new teammates in a new conference and a new division, he remarkably led them to his seventh Super Bowl championship.

Is Tom Brady such a freak of nature that his physical prowess dominates his competition? Not at all. In fact, he was looked over so often in the 2000 NFL Draft that he wasn't selected until the 199th pick during the sixth round. Some say that what stood out for Brady is his vision. Others say it was his poise. He's also been credited as being patient, intelligent, and a student of the game. I would offer a different take, however.

I was fortunate to have been on the sidelines during a half-dozen of his most memorable playoff performances. I was about twenty yards away from Brady when kicker Adam Vinatieri kicked the winning field goal as time expired, giving Brady and the Patriots their first Super Bowl championship in New Orleans in 2002. During the infamous Deflategate game, one of those "deflated balls" rolled to me on the sidelines, and I handed it to the ref. And no, I didn't squeeze it to see if it was deflated. I also shot images of him dismantling the Colts (multiple times), Steelers, and other AFC contenders during their two decades of playoff dominance.

But at the end of the 2017 AFC Championship Game in drizzly Foxborough, Massachusetts, I noticed something astonishing. The Patriots had just defeated the Pittsburgh Steelers to advance to yet another Super Bowl. I was on the field, photographing the celebration between the players, with a mix of family, friends, and media swirling together. It's a chaotic scene to say the least. I jammed my way over to the podium where Brady and the Patriots would receive their trophy.

As Brady approached, I turned around to see rock star Jon Bon Jovi directly behind me, New Kids on the Block singer Donnie Wahlburg to my left, and actor Joe Manganiello next to Wahlburg. Somehow, I finessed my way into the VIP area next to the podium where only a handful of people were allowed. For one brief moment, it was only me, Brady, and Patriots owner Robert Kraft. They embraced in a big hug as I shot away. Moments later, former teammate Teddy Bruschi entered the area to congratulate Brady.

It was there that Brady showed why he is different from the rest. As Brady was being asked to step up to the podium to receive all the praise and accolades in front of millions across the world, he leaned into Bruschi to say something. What I heard wasn't about Brady, and it wasn't about football. It had nothing to do with what any of us might be thinking if we were in his position at that moment.

Brady asked about how one of Bruschi's kids was doing. They then discussed some details, and Brady explained how he wanted to help. After that conversation ended, he turned to step up on stage. I walked to the other side to get a better angle, but I kept thinking about what I just witnessed. It was hard not to be completely impressed by Brady's curiosity about Bruschi and his family. After winning one of the biggest games of his life, getting ready for the Super Bowl, how was his mind not consumed with everything he had just done or was about to do? Why was he so curious about Bruschi and his family, years removed from having been a teammate?

When Brady arrived in Tampa, he continued to surprise the world. It would be easy for the greatest player of all time to pull rank and possess a giant ego. Instead, he took the opposite approach.

He reached out to each of his new teammates. Apparently, this is not uncommon. New teammates were always surprised by what would happen upon their arrival in New England. Brady was the star and everyone knew his name, yet he always made sure to introduce himself to the new teammate, with a "Hi, I'm Tom." As if they didn't already know. His curiosity to get to know his teammates—both the stars and the newcomers—endeared him to each of them.

In fact, Brady asked for only one thing upon signing with Tampa Bay. It wasn't for a specific jersey number. It wasn't for control of the offense. The one thing he asked for were the phone numbers of each player on the team so he could contact them personally.

Initiate the Conversation

"The best ideas start as conversations." — JONATHAN IVE

Curiosity is powerful. So powerful that it can help force action.

Nine years after meeting Funzi, I was in the early stages of my quest toward the world of journalism. I took a rare day off to enjoy some sunshine by rollerblading in New York's Central Park. It was a glorious afternoon—until I smashed into a car while rolling full speed downhill. The impact sent me flying heels over head, spiraling over the freshly dented car. I crashed onto the asphalt, skidding to a stop with the Guggenheim Museum upside down in my blurry vision.

My career path was put on hold for a month as I recovered.

Weeks later, bored out of my mind, my dad saw an ad in *Newsday*, my hometown paper and, at that time, the sixth largest daily paper in the country. The ad described a presentation by their photographers, who would be showcasing their work and taking questions from the public. *Becoming a Newsday photographer was my dream job.* I knew I had to go. So I hobbled my bruised body into their auditorium and sat quietly in the back.

To my surprise, the MC that evening was Jim Dooley, the Director of Photography at *Newsday* and the husband of my photography teacher, Sue Dooley. I needed to meet him. Yet I was too shy and intimidated to ask any questions.

When the presentation ended, I quickly got up to leave. But as I was walking toward the door, something stopped me and forced me to get over my fears.

I turned around. Taking a deep breath, I walked to the front row. I waited impatiently as Dooley talked with a handful of people looking for his attention. It was finally my turn, and I blurted a quick mumbling of admiration.

"Mr. Dooley, I'm a huge fan of your newspaper," I said quickly. "I'm a student in your wife's class, and I just wanted to say hi and introduce myself."

"Vincent," Dooley said with excitement. "Sue has told me great things about you and your work ethic. This is perfect timing. We have a student internship that we haven't filled yet. It's two days a week. If you want it, come by my office on Monday with your portfolio."

I thanked him and walked out of the auditorium, with less worry and more opportunity. I showed up Monday morning in awe. I got to the building early and walked the hallways, staring at the giant photos on the walls. Intimate moments with former presidents, famous athletes, celebrities, inventors, and everyday heroes. I couldn't let the opportunity slip. It would be a chance I'd never had before. Dooley thumbed through my portfolio and let out an occasional smile that gave me hope I would land the gig.

Twelve days later, with a *Newsday* press pass around my neck, I walked past the crowd and directly onto the football field for my first sports assignment. I stood on the sidelines and looked at the pass. That pass read "All Access," giving me free rein to go wherever I wanted on the field, in the press box or the locker rooms.

The next morning, I rushed to grab the paper with the excitement of a child running downstairs Christmas morning. I grabbed the Sports section and flipped through until I finally saw it on page B 23. My image, with my name printed underneath it. I looked up and realized that a publication with my image was being delivered to nearly 600,000 people in New York that morning. I mean, Madonna, Jerry Seinfeld, or Derek Jeter could be seeing it! Yeah, I'm embarrassed to write what I thought.

That was the start of a twenty-two-year career that surpassed any and all expectations. And it's likely that none of it would have occurred if I had walked out without initiating a conversation.

Jim Dooley certainly wasn't going to walk up those steps to offer me that internship. It was up to me.

How often are you walking away from life-changing opportunities because you are more afraid than you are curious? It's so easy to talk ourselves out of initiating a conversation because we are afraid of looking stupid. It's easier to just walk out quietly and say it's not the right time, you didn't know what to say, or that you didn't have the right question to ask. But let me give you a tip: if you put yourself in a position where you have no choice but to ask a question, I guarantee you that you will not only figure out the right thing to say, you will force yourself to come up with a great question.

That experience with *Newsday* helped me create my own rule for events I attend. I have to sit in the front row if possible, and I have to ask one question if allowed. That one is nonnegotiable. I am surprised by how many people leave these opportunities on the table. I assure you that as soon as you commit to this, your demeanor immediately changes. Instead of drifting off and finding reasons why you can't come up with a question, you will scan your mind and come up with something great. Going back to the story that started *The Wealth of Connection,* Seth Godin never would have introduced my book to his audience if I hadn't raised my hand, asked a question and initiated that conversation.

This is a practice. It's a mental muscle that we must flex. I have gotten infinitely better at initiating conversations—often on the fly—because of my conference method. And no matter what field you are in, this skill makes you more interesting, likable, and appreciated.

Appreciated, you ask? Absolutely. See, you are nervous being in the crowd. You are on that Zoom call trying not to make a fool out of yourself. But how do you think the host or the speaker feels? Beyond their cool, curated outer shell, do you think they are nervous that nobody is going to have any questions and they will be standing there in uncomfortable silence? Do you know how much easier you make their job by asking a question, even a basic one? You allow them to shine. You validate their platform. And you create a new connection.

Some of the most valuable collaborations began this way. And if you can, ask the *first* question. You help the leader set the tone, which often prompts them to seek you out and thank you, while making a good impression on everyone in the room. I can't count the number of times people—including the speaker— have thanked me for asking a certain question. Some of the most influential friendships in my network began by me asking an interesting question while they were on stage-either in person or virtually.

The Conversation That Never Happened

"A conversation is a dialogue. Not a monologue. That's why there are so few good conversations: Due to scarcity, two intelligent talkers seldom meet."

— TRUMAN CAPOTE

I thought back to a conversation with my guidance counselor early in my high school journey. She matter-of-factly laid out my future career options. She went on to explain what I was not capable of doing and which avenues would be more suitable. It was all so demoralizing and uninteresting. Looking back, it doesn't surprise me that I never cared. Why would I care to learn something I wasn't interested in to begin with?

That conversation took place a few months after I met Funzi. I thought about how my life and my school experience would have been different if my education were geared toward passionate interests instead of a structured and narrow curriculum. I thought of what my dad said to me when I was twenty-two.

"You like sports. You like taking pictures. You like traveling. Why don't you become a sports photographer?" he suggested.

What would have happened if my teachers were interested in guiding me toward what I was passionate about and not what they assumed were my only options? What would have happened if they asked questions—like Funzi and my dad did—instead of making statements? I can't help but wonder what would have happened if my teachers, who chided me for caring more about sports than my studies, were curious about *my* interests?

Here's a conversation that never happened.

"Vince, you love sports," the counselor states. "You study it without being asked. We love when students follow their curiosity, and we encourage them to dive deeper into those interests. But we've got to be honest. You probably won't be taller than 5'10". You aren't nearly as fast as you think you are. And I saw you quit the football team because you felt insecure and not good enough."

"You saw that?" I respond, somewhat embarrassed.

"Yeah, we all did," she confirms. "But let me let you in on a little secret. There are many more careers for you besides the limited options presented here. You might not know this, but we can't present all those options because we couldn't keep everyone in line. It would be impossible to control, so we need to put everyone into specific boxes. Plus, we need to feed all these universities with new clients—err, students. Now, I don't want to crush your dreams, but let's confirm that you aren't going to be a professional athlete. Are you cool with accepting that?"

"It's pretty obvious," I say, dejectedly nodding.

"With that said," she continues, "did you know that you can still have a career you love where you have almost complete access to that world?"

"No," I responded curiously. "Nobody ever mentioned it."

"Oh, yeah," she begins to explain. "Do you realize how many careers are built around that world you could be great at? There are sportscasters, writers, statisticians, public relations, management, agents, trainers—even the grounds crew! They are all based around sports. Have you ever thought about being a photographer? They *literally* get paid to be on the field with the players. They get to take the pictures that go into magazines, newspapers, and trading cards. And they feed you! It could be your dream job!"

Now, that conversation never happened. Instead, I was told to be an accountant. But I will tell you that if that conversation had happened, I would have been like a cannonball shot out of a cannon. I would have been the best student at Roslyn High School. Instead, I was possibly the worst student at Roslyn High School.

Being Shy Is Being Selfish

I've gotten better at not making people feel uncomfortable with my shyness."

—CLEA DUVALL

When I was four years old, my parents took my brother Steve and me to a birthday party. My parents were friends with the family, but my brother and I didn't know anyone. I was shy and nervous as we pulled up to the party, keeping to myself as my older brother jumped out of the car. He was more outgoing, and he showed it by running ahead of all of us into the party.

"Where are you going?" my mother asked him as he ran ahead.

"I'm going to play with my friends," Steve responded.

"What friends?" my confused mother asked.

"The friends I'm going to make!" he yelled back.

The next thing they knew, he was playing games with a bunch of kids. As Steve ran into the crowd, what did I do? I went off on my own because I was shy and was worried about what shy people worry about: themselves. I was embarrassed thinking about what others might say. Maybe they wouldn't like me. Maybe I might look silly doing something. So while my brother played with his new friends, I went and hid.

After some searching, my mom found me way back in the yard. I was sitting underneath a tree with one of those wind up happy birthday musical toys. All alone, I was twisting it as it played the music over and over again. I was singing "Happy Birthday" to myself. My mom loves telling that story because she always joked that, me being the shy one, I would one day move away to California just to be by myself.

It turned out that I was the one that moved away all right, though never to California. Steve stayed and I haven't lived in New York for more than twenty years. But it's a funny and cute story about our personalities back then, which I forced myself to grow out of. Steve is still as outgoing as ever.

I learned that I got attention for being shy. People see the shy person and don't want them to feel left out or hurt, so they go out of their way to make the shy person more comfortable. People naturally don't want others to feel scared or afraid, so they come to help. That was me at that age. I realized that by being shy I was also being selfish because I made everything about me. The way I reacted and responded to others was all about how I was feeling. It was all about my insecurities. I didn't have to be concerned about anyone else.

When I was shy, I was never very welcoming. In fact, I made everybody else work *harder*. I was making other people have a conversation with me. I was making other people think of ways to communicate with *me*; accommodate *me*; make *me* feel better.

It's selfish to be shy. My shyness made them uncomfortable. It made them do things they wouldn't normally do because I was so wrapped up in myself. When you're shy, who are you thinking about? Are you really worried about how you're making other people feel?

You're shy because your focus is on yourself.

So how did I change that? I trained myself to be more interested in what other people are doing, feeling, and saying.

That sounds basic and simple, but think about the conversations you have as an adult. When people talk about themselves endlessly and are not curious or interested in others, that's the opposite of shy—but the result is the same. Whether you're shy or you're talking all the time, it's all about you. It's all about how you feel. But what happens when you can change that to thinking about what others are thinking and feeling? If we actively wonder about what other people are going through, we ask them questions. We want to know how we can better fit in with what they're doing. What are they interested in? The end result is that they're thrilled that somebody is interested in them because so few people actually are.

My friend Chris Niemeyer does this brilliantly. His curiosity and his meaningful questions always make me feel important during our conversations. When a person has genuine interest, it shows. And it's impossible to not feel lifted up when someone is truly interested in knowing more about you. Chris is one of those guys that, whatever he does, it seems to always be met with success. From afar, people can say he's just lucky. But his character and curiosity combine to form the foundation for true connection.

If you say that you're shy or have a hard time connecting with people, think about this for a minute: you might just be selfish. And the reason why it's not working is because you're so worried about what you're going through or or how you will be perceived that you're not thinking about how you can connect with others. If you start being curious about what's going on in their lives and put the focus on them and less on you, you'll see your relationships build quicker. You'll see your business build quicker and your insecurities go away because it's really not about you.

Ask Better Questions

"Without a good question, a good answer has no place to go."
— CLAYTON CHRISTENSEN

Asking questions is becoming less common as society devalues curiosity. Even just asking "why" is a step up from what many of us do. But to reach a higher level of curiosity, we need to learn to ask better questions.

"Why" shows that you are thinking. But if we don't go further, it's possible to get stuck as a problem creator and not a problem solver. "Why" opens the door to opportunities. It peels back the layers from surface answers to what the real problems are. After you ask why three times, you know a lot more about the struggles than asking just once. For example, take the out-of-shape person who states they know they need to exercise.

"Why haven't you been to the gym?" the curious person asks.

"I just don't have any time," comes the response.

Now, it would be easy to leave it there. It would be easy to empathize and not push any further. But the truly curious can't leave that answer alone. Anyone who really is concerned would like to know more.

"Why don't you have time?"

"Well," they respond, "it's not really that, I guess. I have time. I'm just so busy with the kids, with work, that I don't know where to fit it in."

"Okay," the curious one keeps on. "Why can't you work out first thing in the morning before the kids get up?"

"Ugh. Yeah, I know that's probably the thing to do. I haven't made it a priority or created a schedule to make it happen. I do know that when I was more structured, I was able to work out and read a little before the kids got up."

What started as not having time led—after three whys—to a real answer to the problem. Without the whys, they would continue believing something that wasn't true.

Once we get past the whys, the better and more productive questions come from the hows. Now that we know why it isn't getting done, the hows allow us to figure out how to do it.

"How can you create a schedule to exercise in the morning?"

"How will you stick to your schedule?"

"How will you feel after you work out?"

All of this progress—which can happen quickly—comes from curiosity. It comes from being interested, engaged, and considerate regarding what someone else is going through.

Yet, when we train generations from a young age to lose their curiosity, we lose our empathy. We lose our interest in others. We lose our basic ability to be curious. We don't know what to say or how to say it. Instead of creating an engaging conversation that helps others while energizing ourselves, we do the very things that make people become less attached and attracted to us, which leads to worse relationships and less successful careers.

As our curiosity fades, so does our ability to connect, solve problems, and interact better, which often leads to a lifetime of loneliness, disconnection, and missed opportunities—opportunities we'll never even know we lost.

Curiosity Markers

"Curiosity will get you further than confidence and answers."

— MAXIME LAGACE

The idea of the starving artist is not far from the truth. Some of the best artists I know struggle when it comes to money. They don't like to charge for their services. They feel like they are taking advantage of others by charging because they don't value their own work.

Yet there is the rare artist who does their art in a unique and honest way. They add so much value to their followers and make a wonderful living doing so—allowing them to thrill their audiences even longer.

Freddy Mercury, the lead singer of the band Queen, was one of the rare ones. The band's chart-topping success led them to become high-grossing artists while infusing endless creativity into a style that was uniquely their own. It's a blend that any artist in any field would crave. Most don't like to sell, and they don't know how to promote their unique art without coming across as a sleazy salesperson.

Mercury and Queen figured that out. But when many people see just what the highlights and documentaries show them, there is always more to the secret sauce than meets the eye. Although supremely talented, Mercury was always looking for a special way to connect with audiences. They are now revered for their classic performance at Live Aid in 1985, where they performed among the most popular musicians at the time. Queen was largely an afterthought on the bill after most of the music world determined their best days were behind them. But from the moment they hit the stage, Mercury had the audience in the palm of his hands.

Through all their years onstage, Freddy Mercury paid close attention to how to connect with an audience. Mercury went into shows—no matter where in the world—with immense curiosity about the local language and culture. When he went into a remote country where he didn't know the language, he studied phrases so he could connect with them.

One of the simple, little things Mercury did on tour in the early days was to bring a black marker with him. He did that so when he came upon a thought or idea he wanted to bring to the crowd, he could write it on his arms. In between songs, when the timing was right, the flamboyant singer would say something in their language that would make them laugh or show knowledge about the area. This made the audience feel special that someone so successful—someone who had toured the world—cared about them and where they lived. He made them feel seen. That helped the band develop a loyal, faithful following around the globe that brought them megastar fame.

As you think about your career, what little thing can you be curious about that provides a closer connection to your clients or your audience? And before you get overwhelmed, realize that hardly anyone takes the time to do anything like this. So even the smallest gesture can go a long way toward making a deeper connection.

Everyone Knows Something You Don't

"A mistake that makes you humble is better than an achievement that makes you arrogant." —ANONYMOUS

The problem with success is that it entices us to lose our curiosity. When you are doing well and are lavished with praise, it's difficult to maintain the curiosity that propelled you to success. In the beginning, we know that we need to learn. We need to figure things out, otherwise we won't survive. Well, at least our dream won't survive.

But success can be a terrible teacher. Arrogance is rare in the underachiever unless it's met with delusion. But once success is tasted, it can be easy to believe that we have it all figured out. So often, we wonder how those who had everything let it all slip away. It can be blamed on arrogance. It can be pinned on ego. But what happens is the curiosity that brings them there leaves after they arrive.

When we're hungry, we know we can learn something from anyone. There is a terrible saying that says, "never take advice from someone you wouldn't trade places with." I know what was meant when that was said, but that quote smacks of an arrogance that will hurt most anyone who follows it. And too many people follow it.

It's a selfish way of looking at the knowledge that others can share. It's saying that because you aren't currently where I want to be, your advice is not valuable. Yet, the best advice often comes from those people.

I mentioned Tom Brady in an earlier story. He is arguably the greatest quarterback of all time. Yet, he had a head coach he took advice from. The same with his offensive coordinator. And during many of his Super Bowl years, a quarterback coach too. Now, would Tom Brady trade places with any of them? Would he give up his mansions, his supermodel wife, his celebrity, and his boatloads of cash to trade places with any of them? I would guess no. Yet he listened, learned, and grew by taking advice from the very same people he wouldn't trade places with.

There is a wealth of knowledge and wisdom within swaths of the population we don't value. When we falsely believe that we can only learn from those who are currently in a higher position than us, we disregard beneficial insights from those who may have *already* done what we want to do, or who have experience in a different area that adds a new perspective in the field we are in.

There is value in going outside your current industry to learn. In our *Total Life Freedom Mastermind Community,* we intentionally bring together a blend of entrepreneurs from a wide variety of industries and positions simply because that diversity adds a richness that wouldn't be shared if we all came from the same field.

As knowledgeable as we might be in a particular area, we are always clueless in others. The person who is amazing at personal communication often doesn't have a clue about how to automate their work or how to do anything efficient with technology. The person with extreme talent at the beginning of their career can gain worldly knowledge from older people who were once in their shoes.

We need to shield ourselves from the arrogance of thinking that the only people who can help us are people already doing what we want to do. Every person knows something that we don't.

Do You Chase Efficiency or Exploration?

"Jobs fill your pockets, but adventures fill your soul." — JAIME LYN BEATTY

In the early 1900s, the United States was changing at a rapid pace. One of the areas that was transforming our nation was the invention of the automobile. But these cars were slow, clunky, and highly customized. Every part needed to be custom built, making cars an expensive toy for the wealthy.

Henry Ford changed that. The introduction of the automobile changed the way people worked, lived, and traveled. But its impact on the business world was just as big. With the mainstream establishment of the assembly line, Ford changed the way business was done. Instead of taking twelve hours to build a car, he was able to reduce that to a little over ninety minutes. The methodic work of having employees do a single task allowed for maximum efficiency throughout the company.

But the workers got bored quickly. They began leaving the Ford Motor Company for competitors because the work was so monotonous and the pressure consistent. Ford had a dilemma. So he did something that many thought would bankrupt the business. He enticed his employees to stay by doubling their wages. And instead of going bankrupt, he attracted numerous workers to Detroit. The company's efficiency allowed the mechanics to work fewer hours while earning more money.

The assembly line led to a new era in the United States of mass production, faster turnaround times, and cheaper products. Efficiency took over—from schools to office jobs and everything in between. All that progress, though, means we have rapidly gone from a nation of explorers to a nation looking to make things as efficiently as possible.

I wonder what happened to those employees who didn't return to Ford. The ones who didn't chase money and better hours. They left for a reason—the work was boring. Yet, many returned, and many more flocked to the assembly line once the pot was sweetened. They traded their creativity, curiosity, and freedom for a bigger paycheck and fewer hours. More than one hundred years later, that pull is stronger than ever.

I can't help but wonder how many innovations and inventions were abandoned for the allure of efficiency and safety. The enticement of the steady paycheck has killed more dreams than anything else.

So what are you chasing? Are you chasing the safe, sure thing that guarantees food on the table and the lights staying on? Or is the idea of exploration and freedom so strong that you can't imagine giving that up for work that kills your curiosity and creative ideas?

What Does This Button Do?

"All growth is a leap in the dark, a spontaneous unpremeditated act without the benefit of experience." — HENRY MILLER

I remember clearly the first heavy metal concert I went to. I was fourteen years old when I went with some friends to see Iron Maiden. That evening, sitting in the upper rows of the cigarette- and marijuana-filled air of the Nassau Coliseum, I was transfixed from the moment the band appeared. They hit the stage with a flurry, launching into their song "Aces High," but only after a dramatic introduction that featured Winston Churchill's inspirational "Never Surrender" speech from World War II. The band captivated me from the moment the first song started.

The next day, I began listening to more of their music, studying the lyrics and, to my surprise, learning. They were different than the sex, drugs, and rock and roll bands of the '80s. Their lyrics were stories about history, touching on the flight of Icarus, ancient times, and the nuances of war. They helped me become interested in history—something that my high school classes never did.

Bruce Dickinson, the lead singer of Iron Maiden, is just as interesting as their music. Aside from being the lead singer of one of the biggest metal bands in history, he is a world-class fencer, a brewer, and a 747 pilot. In fact, on one Maiden tour, he was the one who flew the plane to and from all of their gigs—allowing them to store the band, crew, and cargo on a single plane. That allowed the band to perform in cities most bands never get a chance to play.

On top of all of his skills and accomplishments, he is an author. His book, *What Does This Button Do?*, is an appropriate title for the way he takes life in. Oozing with curiosity, Dickinson is always looking to see what the next challenge is without being afraid to push the buttons needed to get there. With fencing, he worked tirelessly to become a decent right-handed fencer, but he didn't think it felt right. So he switched hands and became a champion left-handed fencer. Most of us don't attempt to write with a different hand, let alone learn to fence with it and become a champion. That curiosity is what has allowed him to live such a creative, complex, and fascinating life filled with richness, adventure, and accomplishment.

Yet as the curious know, many people simply don't get it. Most people have had their curiosity beaten out of them for so long that they don't understand the mindset of the curious. When *What Does This Button Do?* was published, the German publishers couldn't understand the title. Being an engineering culture, they couldn't grasp the idea of asking such questions. *What Does This Button Do?* was too uncertain to have as the title. As Dickinson explained, they wanted the title changed because nobody is going to push a button without first knowing what it does.

To Dickinson, that was the exact point. When guests entered the cockpit of the 747 before a flight, they always asked what each button did. He said it was the perfect metaphor for his life. Yet years into his time with Iron Maiden, Dickinson became terrified because he realized he had no idea how to be creative outside the framework of that band. So he quit. The singer acknowledged that anything he has ever created that was worth a lick happened when he was hanging by a thread, uncertain if he would make it. He concluded that the secret was in pushing the buttons only when he had no clue what they did.

What is unleashed when taking a leap in the dark is the endless childlike curiosity we used to have. If you wait to push the button until you know what it does, you will lose all the potential for growth that comes from your life.

What does that button do? Push it and find out.

Are You Interesting or Interested?

"The secret of the man who is universally interesting is that he is universally interested." —WILLIAM DEAN HOWELLS

Being a keynote speaker is a fascinating study in psychology. If you aren't careful, it can be easy to get so wrapped up in what you are speaking about, how you present, and how your message will resonate that you forget that people want to be heard more than they want to be talked to.

I was slated to give a speech that would be the closing keynote for a conference, but I thoroughly enjoy the atmosphere of listening to the other speakers, and more importantly, meeting the people at the conference. So anytime I get the opportunity, I stay for the entire event to take it all in. This conference was set up where I had the ability to sit down at different tables and get to know the attendees in between presentations. There is a certain amount of ego that can come with being the headliner at an event, yet I learned a great lesson that day.

When I approached the first table, I was recognized immediately. Before they asked me a question, I asked what they were trying to figure out for themselves. Suzie's eyes opened, and she jumped on the opportunity. The only reason the conversation ended was because the next speaker was introduced. During the next break, and the subsequent breaks after that, I intentionally went to different tables but asked the same question. There is something about simply giving someone the ability to talk that makes them feel special.

As the last break wound up and I began to prepare for my keynote, I realized that I hadn't talked about myself the entire day. And not one person asked me a question even though I was one of the main people they came to hear. I walked outside to grab a glass of water and to look over my notes, but I was fascinated by what had just transpired. For a few moments, I doubted my spot as the keynote. Nobody seemed excited to ask me anything. I began to wonder if I was interesting enough to be put in that position.

As I walked toward the ballroom, an older lady at the last table grabbed me by the hand.

"You were such an interesting person to talk to," she declared.

I was taken aback. I barely said anything about myself. All I did was ask questions about what they were trying to figure out. What was so interesting about that? I even joked that I didn't do anything but ask them questions about themselves.

"I've been coming to this conference for years," she said. "I can't remember the last time a speaker came up to us and asked what we were struggling with. Usually, if they do sit at our table, they talk about themselves or what they are going to say onstage. You were so interesting because you were so interested in us."

As I gave the keynote, I was able to improvise and point out people that I had just met when referring to a certain point or lesson. I could see the pride they felt by being pointed out to the crowd. That personal touch would never have occurred without those conversations. I walked onto the stage unsure and walked off with a buzz of connection that I hadn't felt in previous keynotes.

The entire event taught me an unexpected lesson. We try so hard to be interesting so that people connect with our message. Yet it's when we are interested that we become interesting. I didn't need to pound my chest at the table to win people over. Nobody cared. They cared about what they needed to figure out. And my position as speaker— one who asked and answered their questions—was much more valuable to them in that capacity than me talking more about myself. The note I wrote to myself was one I remembered.

Being interested is more impactful than being interesting.

Find New from The Old

"Make new friends but keep the old; those are silver, these are gold."

— JOSEPH PARRY

No matter how positive your mindset, we all get stuck. It could be because we are confused about the direction we are going. It might be because there are too many options to choose from and you feel paralyzed. It often is that we no longer feel challenged. We feel less energized as the creep of complacency kicks in. It's hard to put a finger on why because it moves in slowly. We're confused that the roaring fire that used to be there now feels like a smattering of embers.

Whatever the reason, it's a dangerous spot to be in. When our curiosity turns into certainty, we lose the childlike wonder that makes life so adventurous. We suddenly feel trapped. We don't want to lose what we already have while at the same time don't feel the passion we once felt.

When I was little, there was a song with a distinct sound that I recognized quickly each time it came through the car speakers. The song was "Escape" by Rupert Holmes. Most people who remember it recognize it as the Piña Colada song.

I've always been interested in lyrics because I get lost in the storytelling. "Escape" did it when I was a kid, and I still learn from it when I hear it today. The story is about a man who has grown tired of the woman he's been with. He concludes they have just been together too long. While she sleeps, he picks up the newspaper and glances at a personal ad. This woman is looking for a man who likes piña coladas and getting caught in the rain, among other things. He gets excited reading this and responds to the ad stating that he likes all the things she mentions. He sets up a date with this adventurous woman and waits with excitement at a local bar.

At last she walks in. He knows who she is instantly. It's the woman he has grown bored with. She has also felt stuck and bored despite loving the same things as him. It's interesting that not only do they each fade in pursuing what they are interested in, they don't even know what excites their partner.

The song is fictional and based on a "what if" scenario created by Holmes. He reflected later on what he hoped would happen after the couple met up at the bar. Holmes hoped that before the couple went looking for the next fantasy that probably doesn't exist in reality, they would explore their own relationship and invest in their own interests and passions.

When I coach my entrepreneurial clients and they are stuck in their own way, I ask what they loved to do when they were younger. Their answers almost always bring back the childlike enthusiasm that was beaten out of them along the path to being a "responsible adult." There is often so much regret that they didn't pursue those interests.

"Escape" is a simple song that touches many areas of life. Whether it's your career, your relationships, or your hobby, there is gold in finding the new in the old.

If you feel stuck, how can you find the new from the old? Instead of tearing everything down in search of the next unfulfilled (and likely unfulfillable) fantasy, Have you tried getting curious and exploring the nuances of what you already have? Remember what you loved in the beginning instead of starting over again. Reload and reenergize what you have rather than seeking a newer, fresher, more exciting version of the same thing.

Always Be a Beginner

"I love being a beginner. It can be a terrible feeling because you're ashamed of everything you do, but it's so exciting at the same time."

— CHARLOTTE GAINSBURG

There is freedom in being a beginner, and there is stress that comes with success. We see it so often in the world of business. When you reach a certain level, there is a need to maintain or hold on and not fall off. We see it with big businesses all the time. They innovate early on, but when they get to a certain level, they get safe and try not to screw up what they built.

They either get complacent or too scared to change. And that is precisely when the younger, hungrier, and nimbler companies come along and eat their lunch. Because they have the freedom of being a beginner, these small businesses can move quicker and try things bigger companies can't when they are slowed by their sheer size and red tape.

Everyone is striving for this success, but what happens when you get there? Do you get to be as free with the ability to pivot as you do in the beginning? The start is always exciting, but it's also nerve-racking, nauseating and frightening. Yet, you have freedom and flexibility at the start because there are also fewer expectations.

So what are you being a beginner at right now? At all times, I strive to be a beginner at something, intermediate at something and be an expert in something. Right now, I'm a beginner at this book. This project is brand new to me and comes with no guarantee of success. It's a constant, curious study of ideas, concepts, and projections that might not resonate with anyone. Everything that has been successful for us started as a beginner project with no guarantees. The past book, the online course, the mastermind, the community, the speaking, the coaching—all of it. Each one had the exhilarating nausea that my friend Mike Snyder speaks of.

When you are always a beginner, you are bound to make progress. That progress graduates you to a more optimized level and then toward expert status. As you continue, and as projects and businesses elevate, you have income streams on all three levels. And if you always stay a beginner, you will always have a new project idea that requires you to take a chance and grow. What that allows, as income streams stack, is the ability to customize the work you do so you not only have the money you need but also the flexibility that allows you to be fresh, innovative, and excited.

The problems come when we remain in just one category. With our photography business, we eventually graduated to expert status. The money was fantastic and the time needed to do the work was not challenging. We had the freedom that we chased for so long. When we felt bored, we forced ourselves to become beginners again and shifted to an area that was a challenge, like weddings and corporate headshots. The freedom that comes from always being a beginner and always having something we are growing and something we are an expert in gives the ultimate entrepreneurial balance. Because when you take something to the expert level, it gives you what we all want: options.

Once you reach expert status, you can build a team and scale the business to reach greater heights. You can keep it boutique where it's small but optimized, taking up less time yet still earning solid income. You can choose to sell it. Or you can do what we did with our photography business. You have the freedom to kill it. We decided that we didn't want to scale it, we didn't want to stay boutique and keep doing that work, and we hadn't built it the right way to sell it. But because we were always beginners—and had built up options underneath the photo business—we decided it was time to kill it.

Many entrepreneurs eventually become experts, but they don't challenge themselves to be a beginner again. So they have this successful business that makes good money, doesn't take much time and isn't much of a challenge. They are bored and uninspired—all because they are no longer challenged and no longer curious. They have reached that flatlined level of playing prevent defense, simply not trying to lose what they have. They have the money but have lost the excitement.

So I ask you: what are you a beginner in right now that is giving you that energy, that life, and that challenge to grow? What are you doing that comes with a good chance of failure? What are you working on that has no certainty of success? If you don't have it, you might be on a dangerous path toward becoming stuck, and like the man in the song, you need an escape.

Funzi's Legacy

"The idea is not to live forever, but to create something that will."

— ANDY WARHOL

Do you remember Funzi? The scary guy from the bus in New York City that used his superpowers to get me into the Mets game? I never finished that story, did I?

After the game was over, I battled the rush-hour crowds to catch the 7 train, then the Queens bus, then to the N23 that dropped me off down the block from my house. I was looking for him, but I didn't see Funzi anywhere. I ran home as the sun set, darting across the front lawn to tell my parents what happened. I threw open the front door and immediately smelled the sauce that my mom was cooking for our pasta dinner.

My parents had been waiting all day to hear from me, and they were just sitting down to eat. They could barely ask what happened when I started telling them. In between mouthfuls of pasta, I told them everything. I told them about the bus and train, about Funzi from the Waterfront, about Vito, about the food and the program and the banner and the championship rings and Strawberry's home run.

My dad sat there with his mouth open.

"Tell me those guys' names again," he demanded.

"Funzi and Vito," I yelled excitedly!

My brother had a look of envy that was usually reserved for me toward him.

"And where were they from?" my dad asked.

"The Waterfront!" I said, like it was the new Disney World.

It was then that I realized that I needed to tell Scott what happened. So I jumped up from the dinner table, ran two houses down, and in the darkness in front of his house, showed him the program and told him the crazy story.

"Maaaaahhhmmmm!" he yelled, running back in the house to let her know what he just missed. I ran back to my house to finish dinner and the story. My parents didn't hear me come in, but I heard them talking. It was then that I learned from my father how I *really* got into Shea that day.

"He has no idea," my dad told my mom quietly, "that the *mafia* got him into that game."

I went to my room awash in curiosity. For the first time in years, instead of trying to have all the answers, I had so many questions.

How did that happen? Why didn't anyone tell me that these worlds existed? People actually *work* for the Mets? What did Funzi do that allowed him to hang out on a bus on a Tuesday afternoon? How did he know how to help me, and how did he know that guy from the Mets? Why do I have to be in school all day when all of these interesting things are happening outside? Wait…the *mafia*?

The Value of Curiosity

Curiosity changed my life that day. Even though my remaining high school years were torture, it was because I was curious again. I was able to rekindle that endless childhood curiosity. I no longer accepted that I had to do things just because a system told me to so.

Because of Funzi, I began asking questions again. Remember, he did nothing but ask questions until he learned how he could help. It was then that he took decisive action. That brief, fifteen-minute encounter was a crucial moment in my life.

Curiosity means that we initiate the conversation and learn to ask better questions. It means that we know that everyone knows something that we don't and that being shy is being selfish. When you are curious, you are being more interested than interesting, you are looking to find the new in the old, and you understand that you should always be a beginner.

Funzi showed me that being curious was generous. We're told that curiosity killed the cat, but curiosity doesn't kill. Curiosity brings life. It opens doors. It bridges gaps. It gives us permission to see beyond our own limitations and prejudice and pay more attention to what others see. It tells us that we won't know everything. It makes us more likable because we are not trying to be right; we're trying to learn. When we are looking to learn, we open ourselves up to genuine connections. And it's only when we have the ability to create true connections that we can develop the most important aspect of our lives: great relationships.

Part 3

CONNECTION

Value People More Than Ideas

The Connection Business

"Building and repairing relationships are long-term investments."

— STEPHEN COVEY

Ray Kroc, the founder of McDonald's, spoke to a group of college students during the growth of their franchise.

"What business do you think I am in?" he asked the students.

They laughed because it seemed like a silly question.

But he wasn't laughing. Kroc was waiting for an answer.

One student finally broke the silence.

"Mr. Kroc, we all know you're in the hamburger business," the surprised student responded.

"That isn't correct," Kroc responded. "We aren't in the hamburger business. We are in *the real estate business*."

Kroc described how the business model for McDonald's was not about serving high-quality food. I know, you're as shocked as I am! The business model for McDonald's was to purchase as much prime real estate as possible through the McDonald's franchise.

Why does this matter? Because if your business involves dealing with people in any way, you might not be in the business you think you are. *You are in the connection business.*

Business owners struggle because they have been confused by words like networking. To many, networking is going to stodgy events where they hand out and receive business cards, have meaningless small talk with passive people aggressively looking to get something, and listening to pitch after pitch about why the next person's idea is the savior to whatever problem they think you have. So you avoid these events and assume that is what networking is.

Networking and connection are closely tied, so it all starts getting lumped together like a pile of business cards. Yet networking and connection should be thought of very differently. Networking is the act of attempting to gain connections. Often, it is encouraged on a mass scale. In person, it can mean collecting as many business cards as possible (that you will rarely use). On social media, it can mean following as many people as possible, particularly if they are well-known and might be able to help you.

Yet what we crave are deep, meaningful connections. So if you shift your mindset from one who is in whichever business you are in to one who is in the connection business, everything changes. By focusing on the people in your life and not the distractions around you, you develop meaningful connections until you develop a network that is so deep and far-reaching that opportunities will continuously appear out of nowhere.

But if—and only if—you are in the connection business.

Connected Loneliness

"One of the most important things you can do on this earth is to let people know they are not alone." — SHANNON L. ALDER

We are more connected now than at any time in history. Yet we have never felt more alone.

According to multiple studies, nearly half of Americans say that they are lonelier than ever. The age of the internet has thrust itself upon us, and the transition has made some powerful cultural changes on how we communicate. Social media has reconnected us with old classmates and friends while allowing us to form new connections with pretty much anyone we meet. Apps have afforded us the ability to communicate via video or audio on a mass scale at any point throughout our day.

Even though the number of "friends" we have is higher than ever (can you imagine telling anyone 15 years ago that you have 3,000 friends?), our communication skills have dropped faster than we drop friends online for having opposing political views. Although we attempt to pretend like it's real life, it's impossible to truly be real on social media. To see the silliness of how the online world of conversations can be, imagine having lunch with a friend and you state an opinion or fact. From there, you are unable to see any facial expressions from your friend as you wait for a response. As they reply, so can thousands of other people, each one with an opinion and ready to share it. Often, those who are jumping in are people you never met, and if you have, you would never choose to spend time with them.

Real connection comes from real conversations. But you can't have real conversations without discussing real issues and problems. So over time, we build this facade of what we want people to see. Some brag, some complain, and some attempt to be as authentic as possible. Either way, no social media representation is a true view of who that person really is, and individually, we know that. And that emptiness of feeling connected but not really knowing people, and people not knowing who we really are, has led to a river of loneliness.

It's also led to a serious deterioration of our social skills. It's common to get mad at a perfect stranger for their opinion that they never addressed to you personally. We talk (type) to people online in a way we would never think to talk to someone in person. Our ability to read other people's emotions is being damaged as well. A study shows that after five days away from digital devices, kids get better at reading other people's emotions. My friend Josh Brown, the host of the *Franchise Euphoria* podcast, says that if these online conversations were done sitting face to face at a picnic table, 90% of them would lead to deeper connections as opposed to arguments.

In a study from the American Sociological Review, a large percentage of Americans have shrinking networks, fewer friendships, and the average adult male stated that they only have one close friend. And of all of the ills plaguing society, the main reason they seek counseling is for loneliness. So we press on in isolation, diving deeper into the work or individual hobbies that continue on that path. With a shrinking number of trusted friends and a weak network of connections, not only do our personal lives suffer, so do our careers and our finances.

We are missing out on golden opportunities. We are more connected online, but we rarely do anything worthwhile with those connections. We don't nurture them, appreciate them, or harness them like we could. We don't learn more about them because we're too busy judging them on their politics, their looks, or their personal beliefs. We're thinking of the next big thing, not realizing that if our connections were stronger, the next big thing would be easier than ever to achieve. And we'd collectively be a whole lot happier.

A Few Ideas and Endless Connections

"Having too many ideas is not always a good thing." — PAUL ARDEN

A study by the Journal of Nature Communications revealed that the average person has more than 6,200 thoughts each day. That is the *average* person. Judging by how little some people seem to think, I would guess that the average ambitious entrepreneur type has more than 10,000 thoughts per day. Even mixing in a bunch of couch potato days doing nothing but mindless internet scrolling, the average entrepreneur has more than 3,500,000 thoughts per year.

It goes without saying that a good portion of those thoughts will be new ideas. Some of those will be new business concepts, whether solutions for or a new addition to a current business. Since I'm not inside everyone's head—and this is my book so I can do what I want—let's assume that 1% of those thoughts and ideas are new business ideas. I think that number is much lower than what the actual number would be, but let's go with it for simplicity's sake.

That means that every year, the average entrepreneur thinks up 35,000 new business ideas.

Coming up with a new idea is not your problem.

Yet, that's exactly what we think the problem is. We focus on finding the great idea. We spend our time gathering thousands of thoughts in our heads and our notebooks. But great ideas are like the next bus on a busy street. The next one will come along in a minute.

So why do we spend so much time thinking of all of these different concepts? It's because that is what we've trained our mind to do. We've created the wiring in our brain—through repetition—to develop a thought pattern that keeps creating new ideas and thoughts. But is that the thinking that will lead us to success and abundance? I would argue that it's not. I would also argue that we need to train our brains to think more about the relationships in our lives and less about the ideas in our heads.

We need to rewire and retrain our brains to realize that the power of our network is where the opportunities will come. Everyone has ideas, but so few have a great network. Think about this for a moment. After sorting through millions of ideas and finally settling on "the one" to pursue, what do you do next? Do you have any idea where to start? Probably not.

What if you spent your time connecting and cultivating relationships with a wide variety of people from an eclectic group of industries, systems, and geographical areas? What if you knew *everyone* who would be able to help you in every way you can imagine—and many more that you can't? And what if, during those times of relationship-building, you didn't ask for much of anything? You were just a friend, a connector, and a support?

What do you think will happen when you finally do ask for a favor? They will be so excited to help you. Because they know you are a giver, and those givers will be looking for a reason to help you achieve your dreams.

A few great ideas and endless connections are incredibly more powerful than a million great ideas and a few connections.

Read the Room

"You aren't learning anything when you're talking." — LYNDON B. JOHNSON

One of the most powerful ways to form a strong connection with someone is through an engaged conversation. At the same time, one of the quickest ways to turn someone off is by incessantly talking about yourself.

Have you ever found yourself cornered in a conversation with someone who doesn't stop talking about themselves? The person that, no matter how hard you try to change the subject, continues droning on and on? More frighteningly, are *you* that person?

Usually that person doesn't realize that *they* are that person. But what makes someone go on and on about themselves without seeming interested in what the other person has to say? What makes them think that what they have to say is so much more important than anyone else?

They haven't developed the ability to read the room. Reading the room should be a university-level study, yet as a society we pay little attention to it. It is one of the greatest nuanced skills you can develop. To do so requires an emotional understanding of the moods, body language, and reactions of the person you are speaking to. It's being able to understand what people are thinking without them having to say it. It's being able to know when someone is uncomfortable without them verbalizing it. It's knowing when someone wants to say something because their mouth opens a certain way yet they are hesitant to speak. That is reading the room.

I have had people in my life for a long time who have never developed that skill. They do the same things while getting the same results and then get more frustrated as time goes on. The people who don't read the room well don't see the damage they are doing until it's too late. It's one thing to be self-interested when you are young and almost no one has developed those skills. But the inability to develop these skills leads to compounded lost opportunities, damaged or undeveloped relationships, and increased frustration over time. Maybe even a lifetime if you never learn them.

People who have trouble reading the room are usually so entrenched in their own story that they don't attempt to pick up the hints that they have already lost the room. They don't see the wandering eyes looking for a way out. They don't notice the awkward "uh-huh's" or the other person's attempts to bring up a different point. They ignore calculated interruptions and the desperate efforts to get them to stop talking.

I learned this in a difficult lesson. I speak of this person because, like most of these other points, I've been that person. One time I was rambling on, and while in the middle of a story not even close to being finished in my mind, the conversation was briefly interrupted. Before I could get back to the story, the person I was talking to excused themselves from the conversation. I stood there embarrassed, wondering what just happened. It felt awkward knowing that I was dominating the conversation, talking about something they were not at all interested in, and at the first sign of a break, they found their way out of the conversation.

Once you've seen that, it's hard to unsee it. How could I change this? This was obviously not the first time. How often have I done this to others? How many times did I ramble on while the other person didn't care what I was talking about? It was obvious that there were two things that needed to be immediately improved. One, I needed to get better at reading the room. And two, I had to recognize that talkers are often not good listeners. Talkers want to talk. Talkers who don't ask interesting and meaningful questions tend to keep the conversation on themselves, whereas great conversationalists keep the conversation on others. Not only does it make the conversation more balanced, but it makes the other person enjoy talking with you because they feel that you actually care.

The Skill of Listening

"There is only one rule for being a good talker—learn to listen."

— CHRISTOPHER MORLEY

Nick Elkins, a learning architect for Price Waterhouse Coopers and former President for the Association of Talent and Development in Tampa, hired me to give a keynote speech for their annual conference in Florida. I was the opening keynote speaker, and a gentleman by the name of Devon Bandison was the closing keynote speaker. Devon and I hit it off from the beginning, with both of us being native New Yorkers. He was extremely outgoing, talking to people throughout the day in an engaging way. We didn't get to talk much at the conference, but a few months later we reconnected through a phone call.

Few things get me more excited than a great conversation. At times, I get so wrapped up in the conversation that I fail to realize how much I am talking or how often I can cut someone off because I need to get something out before I forget. But being a good talker doesn't mean you are a good listener. Devon taught me a lesson without realizing it.

I noticed right away how helpful he was, curious about what I had going on, and generous in his interests to help and make connections for me. We brainstormed on the state of the speaking world and about running different online communities and events.

But something happened during the conversation that he probably doesn't know I picked up on. Quite often during that talk, we would both talk at the same time. It was one of those humorous situations that happens with people who have a lot to say. But each time we talked at the same time, he stopped talking. Immediately.

The first time, I felt a relief that I was able to get out what I was hoping to say. By the second and third times, though, I felt something different. I was starting to feel selfish as I realized that he stopped talking on purpose so I could continue. This happened a few more times. Each time he paused first.

This was not something I was used to. I grew up in a fast-talking, New York Italian family where you fight for your ability to get a word in. During holiday meals, the chatter coming from all areas of the table was relentless. If you had a point to make, you had to fight to get it in. The quick-moving pace did make for conversational advantages. We were able to tell a story quicker, more comically and with nuance—because otherwise we would lose the room. It forced us to be good debaters as well. We would be eaten alive if we took too long or if our points weren't valid. There was a reason why my dad said that my brother and I should have been lawyers.

The downside is that style of conversation doesn't develop great listeners. The constant focus on getting a word in made for better stories but a deficiency in curiosity. Have you ever been in a conversation where you were just waiting for someone to finish talking so you could say what you wanted to say? Yeah, me too. Those habits have been some of the hardest for me to break, but people like Devon gave me strong examples of not only how to do it, but how good it feels to be in a conversation with great listeners.

The Hour of Giving

"Making money is a happiness; making other people happy is a superhappiness."

— MUHAMMAD YUNUS

I thought about my mentors. The ones I want to emulate. Not for their success necessarily but for their helpfulness. I thought about Funzi and how, in an hour, he taught me more about generosity than I ever learned in school. I mean, one minute I'm alone on a bus looking for a miracle with little money, not a clue, and no connections. And an hour later, I'm sitting in the front row, living my dream, being treated like a king for a day. All within an hour.

So I'm going to talk with you about the one habit change I made that completed the shift from selfish goals to generous goals. I was busy doing what everyone told me to do: create a morning routine to meditate, chart my goals, exercise, and work on my dreams. In other words, a morning routine is all about me. But if I was going to start training myself to think of generous goals, I needed to start over.

So instead of thinking about what I needed, I followed Funzi's path. I would see how I could help people in an hour.

Now, before I created The Hour of Giving I was really good at achieving my goals but woefully inadequate in helping the people around me achieve theirs. It took Funzi less than an hour to help me achieve my dream and leave a lasting impression on my psyche. The Hour of Giving was one of the most transformative steps I've ever created. It increases connection and happiness and builds a powerful network. You have to understand that I fight against structure and routine. If you give me a rule, I will find a way to break it.

When I was five years old, the United States celebrated its bicentennial. Our entire school was decked out in red, white, and blue, wearing the country's colors for the big day.

But I refused.

"I want to wear my green suit," I insisted. "I don't want to wear red, white, and blue."

My parents were exasperated, but I wore them down.

And when the assembly took place, there I was in the auditorium in my swanky green suit with everyone in my class looking as patriotic as ever.

To put it mildly, avoiding structure has been a strength as well as a weakness.

But The Hour of Giving has been so transformative, it's a routine I look forward to keeping.

So here's how it happens. One hour a day was no longer about me. It wasn't about my plans, my goals, or my vision. It was about others. It simply started as sending personal messages to people—usually people I had seen online but whom I hadn't connected with in a while.

It was a little disappointing when some people didn't respond, but many were excited to get the message. So I did a little more of it. That's when things started to shift. My empty inbox filled up. People were so appreciative of getting random messages that they asked what I was up to. I would tell them about how my family was doing, how the kids were growing or that I was going through the pains of writing a book. After about ten people mentioned they would love to read it, I asked if they wanted to read what I had so far. I told them I would love some feedback from someone interested in the topic. Soon, I was sending out the book-in-progress to whomever was interested. That eventually fueled the growth of the book.

There was something about The Hour of Giving that transformed my brain, my heart, and my mindset. Instead of getting wrapped up in me, I began thinking of whom I would reach out to next. It was the little things. With a brief scroll through social media, I realized that so many connections were letting me know what was going on in their lives and what they were struggling with.

They just needed personal connection.

The Hour of Giving then expanded. I realized that I wasn't the only one looking for validation and support. *Nearly everyone was!* They would post a link to their podcast. Hmmmm. What are their goals? So, I'd ask. Near and far, they each wanted two things: for people to share it, and for people to leave a review. It's a pretty easy solution, if I'm in the giving mindset. So doing those things became a part of my Hour of Giving. It wasn't long before this branched out. Oh man, all those books that I've read and loved—I never reviewed most of them. Have I shared them with friends who need them? Have I shared them on social media?

This was the tip of the iceberg. I reached out to people I hadn't spoken with in a while to thank them for what they added to my life. I reached out to people who helped me yet I had never properly thanked. I saw that I could do that for hours a day and not be finished.

The Hour of Giving transformed my life. Not only did it start building and deepening connections, I felt better. I couldn't explain it, but I wasn't thinking about myself that hour. I wasn't wrapped up in my goals, my drama, or my needs. It was all about them. And it felt wonderful.

Keep in Touch

"Don't ignore the effort of a person who tries to keep in touch. It's not all the time that someone cares." — ANONYMOUS

"I've been meaning to reach out to you."

"I was just thinking of you."

"You were on my mind today."

Do you often utter any of these lines?

As a part of The Hour of Giving, I hear those lines often. As well-meaning as those words are, if you have to say them, it means you are too late in reaching out. Yet, those are lines I used to say myself way too often. One of the reasons I started The Hour of Giving was to give the thing I often felt I needed from others. The haunt of loneliness is something that achieving our goals can't erase. If you think that isn't true, explain why so many of the rich and famous turn to drugs and alcohol citing how lonely they feel.

I wasn't rich or famous, but the feeling of being alone is hard to shake. I'm not talking alone merely in the physical sense. I'm talking about being so lonely that you question whether you matter. Those days when you wonder if anyone really cares.

For those who have experienced it, those feelings are indescribable. The emptiness that courses through your body doesn't occur on the good or the great days. It might not even happen on the blah days. But there are those rare days when all you want is to be thought of and reached out to by someone who cares. Someone who doesn't want anything other than to see how you're doing.

On one occasion, I remember sitting on my bed drained of emotion. It was one of the days that I was in my head, turning a little stream into a river. I was filled with self-pity because after contacting a few people who needed help, I was the one in pain. I made subtle hints to let people know I was struggling, but nobody noticed the tiny piece of bait I threw out.

That self-pity led to one of my lost days- where I sit in relative silence, questioning just about everything I'm doing. I felt disappointed that not one person reached out to see how I was feeling. I thought about all of the things that people wrapped up in themselves feel.

I truly believe those were some of the best, most painful days I've ever experienced. Best because it allowed me to develop the empathy to understand what others who struggle with this are going through. It's difficult when you have a positive attitude and good mental fortune to understand what it feels like in those moments. I have frequently lacked empathy. I am a pull-yourself-up-by-the-bootstraps type of person and am not one for excuses. That leads to positive results quite often and less complaining. The downside is it can lead to a hard shell where you forget that others struggle.

The next day, I wondered "*what exactly did I need yesterday*?" What would have taken me out of that funk? And it was clear. I just wanted someone to reach out and ask how I was doing. Was it really that simple? Yes, it was. I didn't need anyone to solve my problems. I didn't want any money. I just wanted someone to care.

Our own pain can lead to the greatest advances in our lives. I wanted someone to do for me what I needed to do for others. I committed to reaching out on a daily basis for no other reason than to check in on friends. Sometimes they are close friends or clients, but many times we barely knew each other. Still, we're connected somehow.

Dedicating that time each day cleanses me of my selfishness. It gets me out of my own head and forces me daily to be a better person. I have countless examples of responses like, "I've been meaning to reach out to you," "I was just thinking of you," and "You were on my mind today." But it's responses like the one a woman named Shari gave me that make it an easy heart-changing habit to continue.

I had checked in on her out of the blue. There was no rhyme or reason for doing so. Just a habit created out of my own pain, but her response hit my heart. She said that she was crying while reading my message. Her husband had just been detained for child abuse the night before. She was confused, alone, and heartbroken for her daughter.

"You have no idea how much you reaching out means to me," she replied. "I've been sitting here all alone, questioning if anyone cares. Your message let me know that the answer is yes."

We continued our conversation over a few weeks while she settled back into life. That message is why I hope to continue doing this every day for the rest of my life.

What Are Your Friends' Goals?

"Most people want to see you doing better, but not doing better than them."

— LONDON MOND

Michael O'Neal is the host of the *Solopreneur Hour* podcast. I listened to his podcast for a year and loved his off-the-cuff, impromptu style of interviewing. Being that he shared his life and interests within the show, I heard him mention multiple times how he is a huge Pittsburgh Steelers fan. I wanted to reach out to let him know that I photographed the Steelers games, but I was a little star struck because I listened to him weekly, and he was friends with big names in the podcast world of entrepreneurs.

I was in San Francisco when I heard him mention his affinity for the Steelers again. It was then when I realized how I could offer value to him and get a chance to connect. I sent O'Neal an email, introducing myself and letting him know about my association with the Steelers. I said that I often get to bring an assistant onto the field for games, and if he's ever interested, please let me know.

He responded almost immediately.

"Interested?" O'Neal replied. "You have got to be joking. Of course I am interested!"

We built a connection and kept in touch for more than two years. When I saw that he was speaking at a conference in Philadelphia when I would be in Washington, DC, to cover the Steelers opening day game, I reached out to let him know I had a press pass for him if he could make it.

It took him less than an hour to push his flight back a day.

The look on his face as we walked down the tunnel onto the grass at FedEx Field was priceless. O'Neal turned into a little kid right before my eyes. He must have thanked me a thousand times and took full advantage of the evening, including tracking down Steelers head coach Mike Tomlin before he got onto the team bus for a selfie after the Steelers victory.

Walking back to the car, he asked me about my book that was going to be released the following year.

"Any introductions that you need me to make, just ask," O'Neal replied. I told him that what I really needed was different podcasts to be interviewed on. I didn't know anyone. We set up a time to brainstorm a few days later. During the conversation, as he listed some podcasters he would connect me with, he asked what I was doing the following day.

"I want to have you as a guest on *The Solopreneur Hour*."

To have my first podcast interview be on a show that was not only one of my favorites but one with a huge following, was an amazing start to this new world I was building. But it didn't start with me trying to get O'Neal to have me on the show. I didn't have any following or platform, but I had access to a world he loved and didn't have access to. I didn't do it to get onto his show. I never thought he would make that offer. I just wanted to offer that experience for him. That interview got me five other interviews from other podcasters, and those were the seeds that opened doors to me being interviewed more than 125 times for my book. There is no way that it would have been as fast and expansive without that boost from O'Neal and his show.

If I focused on my goals and mine alone, I would have done like everyone else: pitch him to be a guest on his show. He told me that night that he gets endless pitches from people and agencies, and he throws most of them away. But when he has a personal connection he finds interesting, he doesn't hesitate to bring them on. Being focused on his goals without any expectations for myself actually got me what all those chasing selfish goals can't get.

What's in a Name

"Remember my name and you add to my feeling of importance."

— DALE CARNEGIE

I have been historically atrocious at remembering names. I mean, a world-class level of horribleness. I'm not sure if it's because I get so wrapped up in conversations that I forget or because a piece of my brain doesn't function, but it's common for me to forget someone's name moments after hearing it. Yet I've always been drawn to people who remember *my* name.

While writing this book, I escaped the noise of our homeschooling house to retreat to the local Panera Bread, cozy up in a nook in the corner, and get a few hours of silent writing in. Being fully engrossed in the writing process, I had forgotten to grab lunch. I naively left my computer on the table, trusting the businessman sitting to my left with making sure nobody took it. I was incredibly hungry but didn't want to pack up all of my stuff. That would have been the story I'd be writing about if that experience went poorly.

I ordered my Thai Chicken Salad, casually gave my name, and went back to the table to resume my writing. The salad was delicious as usual, and I spent the next three hours working on the book and other business-related tasks. At some point, I felt the urge to grab a refill for my unsweetened iced tea, but they were out.

The gentleman behind the counter took it upon himself to make sure a new batch of tea was made. Minutes later, I looked up to see him headed toward my table with a smile on his face and a full cup of tea in hand.

"Here you go, Vinny!" he declared enthusiastically.

I thanked him but was confused. I never gave him my name. I was positive that I only mentioned the tea. There was no reason to say my name. And the last time I gave my name was hours before when I ordered my food. I glanced at my receipt to see that he was the one who took my order then. And somehow, after serving probably a hundred customers over that time, hearing countless names and orders, he remembered the name of a guy from earlier in the day.

I got back to writing but glanced up often to watch his interactions with other customers. He didn't appear to do anything different than his coworkers. Same hustle, same attention, same speed. Despite having gone to this Panera for years, I never felt "special" before.

As I packed my bag to wrap for the day, I couldn't leave without saying something to him.

"I have to ask," I said. "Why did you remember my name?"

"Oh," he said, seeming surprised and grateful for the question. "I just think that remembering people's names is a great way to make them feel special."

Extensive research shows that he is spot on. Dale Carnegie, author of *How to Win Friends and Influence People* says, "Remember that a person's name is to that person the sweetest and most important sound in any language."

It turns out that the most important word in our vocabulary—at least in our own brain—is our name. Yet, I am not alone in forgetting. Kai Stabell, the founder of the Consortium for Conversational Conflict Resolution, says that one of the main reasons so many people are bad at remembering names is that people normally tell you their name when you are least ready to absorb it. Stabell explains that when we meet someone, we are processing, identifying, and noticing so much stimuli that we tend to forget the simple things like someone's name.

I wasn't looking for an excuse as to why I was so poor at this, but he gave me a good one. When we meet someone new, we often stop what we're doing, figure out how to introduce ourselves, attempt to be conversational, and if we are with someone else, think of how and when to introduce them. So, faced with all of those challenges, we forget to remember names even though it's one of the most important things we can do to create a deeper connection.

We all want to feel special, and one of the ways we feel most special is when someone says our name. It makes us feel respected and valued. We feel a greater connection with someone who uses our name compared to someone who doesn't. Just like social media comments, we get a hit of the feel-good hormones like serotonin and dopamine when we hear our name. When that happens, we feel unconscious signals like trust, empathy, and compassion in our brains. This is exactly what that employee at Panera did for me. A random stranger made me feel important just by remembering and saying my name.

And I would love to tell you the Panera guy's name and to share it with the world, but I forgot it immediately.

Name Names

"Giving credit where credit is due is a very rewarding habit to form. Its rewards are inestimable." — LORETTA YOUNG

I watched a speech by actor Matthew McConaughey, who has played characters in such films as *The Wolf of Wall Street*, *Failure to Launch*, *Magic Mike,* and many more.

The speech was from the Oscars, when McConaughey won Best Actor for his performance in the film *Dallas Buyers Club*. Even though I had never seen the movie, I somehow found this clip a few years back. It's not often that an acceptance speech draws my attention, but this one did.

He tells the crowd that there are three things he needs every day: something to look up to, something to look forward to, and someone to chase. It's a speech that can force you to think more about yourself than of him while you are listening, which I believe was the goal.

When he discussed someone to look up to, he mentioned God for giving him opportunities he wasn't responsible for, and he mentioned how he was shown that it's a scientific fact that gratitude reciprocates. I heard this speech for the first time in 2015, and that line set me on a path to study gratitude deeper. When he discussed what he looked forward to, McConaughey smoothly credited his dad, who has passed, for showing him how to be a man. He thanked his mom for demanding that he and his brothers respect themselves, and because of that, they were more prepared to respect others. And he got choked up as he thanked his wife and kids. "You are the four people that I want to make most proud of me." Those words inspired my thank you to my wife and kids inside *Freelance to Freedom*.

And then he mentioned his hero. The person that he chases.

And I love the speech, but this is where it drives me crazy. McConaughey said that when he was fifteen years old, he had a very important person in his life ask him who his hero was. He asked for a little time to think about it. This same person came back a few weeks later and asked who his hero was again. That time, he was ready with his answer.

"It's me in ten years," McConaughey said.

Ten years later, he explained that this same person asked him if he was his hero.

"Not even close," McConaughey frustratingly exclaimed. This person asked why.

He said because his hero is him at thirty-five.

He realized that every day, he does what he has to do to get better to become his hero, but he will never catch it. He'll never get there. And he accepts that because it gives him someone to chase.

I loved that message, and I have followed his advice. But something bugged me about it. So I watched it again. And the third time I watched, I finally figured out what bothered me.

Although he gave credit to his dad, his mom, his family, and many others in the speech, the oversight of mentioning the name of the person who gave him the hero advice—the cornerstone of the speech—annoyed me. It made me think of something that so many of us often overlook.

We don't name names while giving credit.

It's something I've paid close attention to after having this realization. I came to see that I wasn't just annoyed at McConaughey; I was annoyed at myself because I often did the same thing. I would mention an idea from a book but not mention the source. I would speak of advice someone gave me but not mention their name. I realized that this needed to be improved, changed and eliminated.

When we don't give credit by naming names, we are robbing the people who help us gain attention, respect, and notoriety. Not only that, but we make the story about us, not them. Now it's entirely possible that this person told McConaughey to not mention their name in the speech. I don't know the full backstory. But I write this because I've seen it so many times and in so many ways.

Giving credit is a vital aspect of what we all do. We crave receiving it. But giving credit actually makes you get recognized *more*. That's because we recognize those who recognize others. It shows that you value honesty and generosity—two attractive traits. Remember, there is no sweeter sound to our ears than the sound of our own name. Give credit, name names, and make the people who helped into the heroes.

Master the Art of Communication

"The art of communication is the language of leadership."

— JAMES HUMES

After my internship at *Newsday* concluded, I was thrilled to learn that the editors wanted me to stay on as a freelancer. There were no guarantees of work, but the more I proved myself, the more I'd get called upon. Armed with my trusty pager, I eagerly awaited that startling buzz from my belt alerting me to the possibility of work. On the other end of the pager was sports photo editor Chuck Bennett. Bennett, the hip, Southern Californian known for flashy neckties, had an arsenal of freelancers at his disposal.

Having shown promise and consistency, I became one of his top three choices. When that pager went off, I called Chuck as fast I could to see if I nabbed the assignment. I was quick enough that I got a decent amount of gigs. But Ed Betz, my competitor-turned-friend, got the lion's share. As grateful as I was to shoot for *Newsday*, I was annoyed by how often I saw his byline in the paper instead of mine. This continued for a few more weeks, and the frequency of his assignments only increased.

I approached Bennett, trying not to sound annoyed, to ask why Ed was getting preferential treatment over me and the other freelancers. Of course, I really was only concerned with myself.

Bennett smiled, sipped on his tea, and kept his eyes on me the entire time. He held up his phone, and in his surfer style, explained to me how he worked.

"I've got you, Ed, and a few others as my main freelancers. Here's what I do—and it's pretty simple," Bennett explained. "I page three of you at the exact same time when an assignment comes open. The first one who gets back to me gets the gig. It's that simple. Ed just gets back to me quicker. You're next, which is why you get as much as you do. The others get the rest." He took another sip of tea. "The easy answer is this: *Respond quicker*."

The following week, I was getting as many assignments as Ed, making more money than ever, and building a strong portfolio. Interestingly enough, he didn't mention the quality of our work. We were all "good enough" to get what he needed. Chuck Bennett valued the person who got back to him as quickly as possible because it made his job easier. The sooner that assignment was filled, the smoother his job ran. It was a slice of humble pie to see that Ed wasn't being favored, or that the quality of my work didn't matter as much as I thought it did. I spent so much time on improving my art but too little time on the art of communication.

Go Where You Are Celebrated

"Promise yourself today to be just as enthusiastic about the success of others as you are about your own." — CHRISTIAN D. LARSON

In his book, *The Power of Who*, Bob Beaudine gives the argument that you already know everyone you need to know. You might feel you don't have a powerful network because you don't know enough people or you don't know the right people. Bob explains that between your inner circle and the people you are connected to now, you already know everyone you need to become successful. By nurturing these friendships and properly allocating your time within these relationships, you have the inner workings of a powerful network at this very moment.

That book touched on something else that hit home for me. Just because we are connected to someone doesn't mean we should be putting time and energy into certain relationships. This is challenging when it comes to family and friendships that are less than healthy. He explained that *we should go where we are celebrated, not tolerated.*

I'm sure I'm not alone in saying that I've put too much time, energy, and emotion into relationships who either didn't want the best for me or would not have been disappointed to see me fail. At the same time, there were people who were openly celebrating me, pushing for me to succeed, who didn't get enough of my time. It didn't take long to understand where I was celebrated and where I was tolerated. Understand that people you may want to celebrate you might never do more than just tolerate you. Can I tell you how liberating that was for me to read?

For years, I tried to get people who tolerated me to celebrate me. Did it lead to a celebration? No. It led to frustration. I spent my time trying to impress those people while giving less time and attention to the people who actually cared. It didn't matter what I did or what I accomplished; I wasn't going to be celebrated. All the while, I put my attention on the wrong people. Changing this did more for my mental health, as well as my network, than I could have imagined.

It made me realize that I did already know everyone I needed to know. Why? Because the people who celebrated me were interested in helping me achieve my dreams, and it was interesting to find out that the more I dove into those who celebrated me, the more people they seemed to know. Being that we developed a great connection, they were interested—excited even—to open up their network. So instead of trying to convince someone to approve of me, I turned to the people who already approved and would go out of their way to make my life better.

The more I went where I was celebrated, the more success increased, frustration plummeted, and my network grew stronger.

Connect the Unconnected

"All good leaders are connectors. They relate well and make people feel confident about themselves." — JOHN MAXWELL

I've already talked about what Funzi taught me, but in that core set of lessons is an important example of building a powerful network: connecting people he knew to help others. Even in a world of selfishness, memories of his lesson seeped into my thinking.

At the rehearsal dinner for our friends Ken and Kim Thomas, Elizabeth and I were strategically seated with a guy named Brian Franey and his date. Brian was a friend of Ken's since their college days at Georgetown and shared many common interests. They were both long-suffering fans of the New York Mets as I was, so Ken seated us together. Of course, I told the Funzi story. The conversation flowed throughout the evening, and Brian and I became quick friends. Brian, a producer for ESPN, worked in many of the same circles I was working in as a sports photographer.

For the next few years, we periodically kept in touch.

One afternoon, Brian reached out asking for a favor. He was in New York City with Kim and Ken, and they remembered that my brother was a stagehand for Broadway shows. They were taking in a show that evening and wanted to know if my brother had any advice on where to get the best tickets. I shared some information with him and then wondered if I could make their experience a little more memorable. I messaged my brother, Steve, to see if he could line up a backstage tour for *Jersey Boys*, the show he was working on.

Within minutes, Steve messaged back confirming that he got it approved. He gave me the info on where to find the stage door and the time to show up. They were thrilled with the upgrade and went on to have a great night meeting some of the actors and catching a behind-the-scenes view of the show.

Long after that night, our paths would continue to cross on the sidelines of different stadiums throughout the country. Brian knew about a photography project I was working on to photograph in every stadium and arena in the United States.

In 2015, LeBron James and the Miami Heat were going for their third straight NBA championship. I was hoping to get a chance to document a part of it for the project because it was history in the making. To my frustration, every avenue I attempted was closed. None of the outlets I worked with could come through for a credential. It was the most difficult pass I tried to get in my career. The Heat rolled Indianapolis for Game Six of the Eastern Conference Finals against the Pacers and I saw on Twitter that Brian was covering it for ESPN.

I sent a simple text asking if he needed an extra photographer for the game. He responded a few minutes later that a press pass would be waiting for me at will call. With one text, I was able to get a pass that was unattainable.

Two days later, I was two feet away from James as I made the image that I had been desperately attempting to make. No amount of effort I put in got me close to that elusive pass. One text to a friend got me everything I was hoping for.

As we left the arena, I thanked him again.

"I owed you!" he said.

I asked for what.

"I never forgot how you went out of your way to help us get that backstage tour on Broadway. That meant more to me than you realize. And your brother was so helpful to us. I wasn't sure how to help. As soon as you asked, I knew how I could pay you back."

Can you imagine that? I was being paid back for something I forgot I had done. This is the power of connecting the unconnected. You get to help the people in your lives by bringing them together.

They would never know each other if it weren't for you. You get to make both of their lives better while simultaneously making your network stronger. And without even knowing it, you build up appreciation that pays you back in the most unexpected ways.

Find and Deliver

"As the world becomes a more digital place, we cannot forget about the human connection." — ADAM NEUMANN

Few people exemplify the idea of connecting the unconnected like Mark Fujiwara. Fujiwara is a director at Baird and a Certified Portfolio Manager based out of Marin, California. A friend of mine, Gustavo Fernandez, connected us while discussing the concepts behind building a powerful network around you.

It doesn't take long to see how Mark's vision for helping far exceeds his drive for personal success. But helping seems like too weak of a word to describe what he actually does. He doesn't just look to connect. He takes it steps further with a real focus on figuring out what the person's deepest goal is. To become as connected and trusted as he has become requires a vision and heart that most simply do not have. How does he do this?

"To start, I don't assume that I know what people want," he explains. "I had a client who wanted to talk with me, and it would have been easy to assume that he wanted to multiply his net worth. But I like to ask why. Ask and ask, and then ask again. What I found out by asking why was that he actually desired a closer connection with his sons. When you find out what their deepest goal is, you get the opportunity to deliver that to them. When you can do that, you also get what you want."

Mark learned early in life that you can do this only if you build an all-star team around you, giving you connections and the ability and trust to refer key people to people within your network. He saw this firsthand as a teenager as he watched his family's business—the most successful Chinese restaurant in San Francisco—go out of business.

"It failed only because they didn't surround themselves with professionals. From the accountants to the contractors, they weren't vetted and they weren't professional, and it destroyed the business," Mark said. "I knew that if they were introduced to the right people, the business would have not just survived but continued to thrive."

Building his team has been the core of Mark's astonishing success. Through years of what he calls "Find and Deliver," which is his mindset for discovering a person's real desires, he has developed a network so vast that it often takes just one phone call to make a connection that changes their life.

He has built that into the ultimate spider web of connections, a system so developed that no matter what someone is looking for, he has a connection who can help. Across almost all industries and professions, he has focused on developing deep ties and helping people get what they really want.

But it has its pitfalls. He has become adept at finding the fakers. The fakers are those who give just to get. He researches their reputations and examines their body language to see if they are less than trustworthy. He is fully confident that through this process, you will get burned. You will be betrayed. It's a sad part of doing business, but a large number of people do not have honorable intentions. So it does take being burned to develop the skills to detect the fakers.

"Coming from the restaurant industry, I look at the little things. Like, how do you treat the waitstaff?" Mark explains. "If you don't treat them well—if you are dismissive toward people that you think aren't as good as you—that's a sign. The more you can read those signs, the stronger the connections and the network you build will be."

"But if you can help deliver them their deepest goal," Mark concludes, "you get to do what truly matters: to make the world a better place."

Two-Minute Friends

"It's the worst part of seeing old friends: when your rose colored memories become undone by reality." — BRAD MELTZER

The late author and speaker Jim Rohn famously said that we are the average of the five people we spend the most time with. Finding the right people to spend time with is a crucial part of our overall happiness, well-being, and success. Alas, choosing who not to spend time with is just as important. So much of our pain in life comes from spending too much time with the wrong people. There are major challenges in understanding who the wrong people are and having the courage to separate yourself from the ones who aren't a great fit.

Now, let's be clear that it's not always a case of a person being good and bad—there is both in all of us. It's just understanding that certain relationships are not a great fit for the vision you have for your life. And we need to be self-aware enough to know that we aren't a great fit for other people as well. We are all the villains in someone else's story, so this isn't a righteous boastfulness of hierarchy.

But we all have those relationships that leave us drained. Family can be the most challenging simply because there is an obligation to spend time together, often around the holidays, which adds a good amount of stress. Rohn introduced me to a concept that allowed me to gain perspective on how to balance the time we spend with the people who drain us and the people who bring us energy. Without an understanding of how we spend our time, we get frustrated by spending too much time with the wrong people and not enough time with the right people.

This concept is "two-minute friends, two-hour friends, two-day friends, and two-week friends." We all have people in our lives who aren't going away, and we don't want to be so rude as to cut them out completely, although there will be days that we feel like doing so. These are your two-minute friends. Meaning, you can spend two minutes with them and that's about all you can handle. They might be the neighbor you see at your kids' bus stop or run into at the coffee shop. You say your pleasantries, they ramble on about some problem that never changes, complain about their spouse, and never ask how you are doing because they are always talking about themselves. You've spent two hours with them and realized it's way too much time since you either have little in common with or, frankly, can't stand them. These are your two-minute friends. When you know that this is the amount of time that you can happily spend with them, you don't waste your time and energy doing more.

Two-hour friends are the ones who are great to grab lunch with when you can make time. You laugh, talk about old times, catch up about family, work or interests, and leave knowing that it was great to catch up. The relationship is good, but there isn't much of a desire to go deeper. You know that by the end of the get-together, there isn't much more to discuss. You have enough common interests to have a wonderful time and that's about as far as it goes. Understand that there is tremendous value in these relationships. You may find that many of your friendships are of the two-hour variety.

Two-day friends are a more specific type of relationship. Not only do you really enjoy each other, but you can hang out for long periods of time and have much more in common. You can discuss politics without either of you running out of the room screaming. You have common interests that allow the conversation to be deeper, more nuanced, and interesting. You can laugh, joke, and understand each other's humor. You can spend multiple days together and feel enriched and fulfilled by your time together. Again, family is the trickier part. We often spend multiple days with family, and because of that obligation or expectation, we leave feeling more drained than engaged. There is an old saying that having guests in your home is just like fish—after two or three days, they both begin to stink.

And then you have the rarest of the rare: the two-week friends. Not everyone has these, by the way. But these are the people who you can take on vacation for two weeks and not want to tear their faces off. These are those rare humans you can enjoy long swaths of time together. The ones who respect your privacy and space, whom your family loves to be around and whom you look forward to spending extended time with.

Knowing where the people in your life line up will be a huge factor in your happiness and the quality of your relationships going forward. When you realize that you spend two weeks with two-minute friends, or only two minutes with two-day friends, the quality of your friendships will increase while the frustration of spending too much time with the wrong people will decrease.

Be the First or the Last

"Curiosity is, in great and generous minds, the first passion and the last."

—SAMUEL JOHNSON

James Malinchak is the most unfamous celebrity in the world of public speaking. I met him inside a mastermind led by John Lee Dumas of *Entrepreneurs on Fire*, and his story grabbed my attention quickly. Now living in West Palm Beach, Florida, James mentioned that he was raised in a small town south of Pittsburgh. I quickly looked it up, and it turned out that he was raised twenty minutes from where we were living at the time.

We connected, and I was astonished to learn that he was considered a speaking mentor for influencers like Les Brown, Jack Canfield, Leeza Gibbons, Joe Theismann, Brendon Burchard, and a host of other speakers, athletes, and celebrities. Yet, he had done this without becoming famous. It didn't take long to see that he possessed all the attributes of *The Wealth of Connection*: Character, Curiosity, Connection, Collaboration, and Creation. It's hard to fail with those in your blood. I reached out to him to interview him for this book, and what was supposed to be a thirty-minute call extended to two hours.

The knowledge he shared was endless, and he did it so generously.

Each time I gave him the option to end the call, realizing that we had gone over on time, he came back with, "Oh, I've got one more for you!" We were discussing the idea of initiating conversation. He cited what so many people do wrong in connecting with influencers. We both agreed that connecting at live events is a fabulous way to meet the rock stars in our industries. Yet, we often face two problems: One we know of, and one we don't. The issue that we know of is that the "celebrities" that we want to meet are hard to get to. They come offstage and get swarmed by participants. How do we get to them if they are bombarded as soon as they get offstage? And if we do get to them, how do we make an impression in a short time frame?

James explained how he solves both of these problems by telling me the story of how he met original *Shark Tank* entrepreneur Kevin Harrington. Without even knowing the context of this book, his approach validated the concepts of *The Wealth of Connection*.

They were both speakers at a conference, and James wanted to meet Harrington. He planned on introducing himself after Harrington got offstage, but the *Shark Tank* star was immediately surrounded. Knowing what he knows, James waited. Once every other person got their questions in, each one looking for something, James approached Harrington as he left the venue.

After a quick introduction, James stated that he could solve the problem Harrington had.

"What problem do I have?" Harrington asked.

"I heard you on stage," James explained. "You said that you love your work but don't like traveling—how exhausting it is, sleeping in hotels across the country..."

"I did say that—and yes, I don't like that part of this," Harrington acknowledged to Malinchak.

"If I could show you how to book all your speaking gigs in your area, so you can do the work but sleep in your bed every night, would that interest you? If so, I can get on a call with you for thirty minutes and show you how," James boldly stated.

Harrington, who was in a hurry to get to the airport, stopped in his tracks. He offered to give James his phone number, but James refused the offer.

"I don't want your number," he explained. "I'll give you my number. Call me if you're interested."

Less than an hour later, James was on stage when he got a text. It was from Harrington wanting to talk. Because of that conversation, he helped Harrington develop a multi-million dollar deal that gave him the lifestyle he was hoping for. They continued to develop a business relationship and a real friendship.

James learned that most people approach people like Harrington looking to get something. His focus was to find a way to serve. When he heard Harrington say which part of his career he didn't like, James knew he could help. And when you approach someone with a solution instead of a request, you immediately stand out.

There is one other part of this story that is valuable.

"When introducing yourself—if you want to make an impression—either be the first or the last," James explained. "Those are the only two people who are remembered. Everyone else is just a sea of noise. When I saw Harrington walk offstage and get swarmed, I waited. I was going to stick around until the end so he would remember me. Once everyone had gone, I approached him with my solution. Being last and having a solution for his problem—one he didn't know he had—was why that introduction was so successful."

Pay Attention

"Attention is the rarest and purest form of generosity." — SIMONE WEIL

It's the little things that get big attention.

Although we focus on growing the numbers of our social media accounts, it's face-to-face skills that really matter. Especially—most especially—in the beginning. We need to be human before we can be successful. It's old school, but if you can get someone to look up from their phones for more than a second, crack a slight smile, and emit more than a grunt, you've eclipsed the societal norm.

Jonathan Mendonsa and Brad Barrett are the hosts of *Choose FI*, a top-rated podcast about financial independence. In just a few short years, they turned their podcast into a powerhouse that routinely averages a half a million downloads per episode. I was in the middle of writing my first book, and Brad expressed interest in reading an advance copy. After I sent him the draft, he and I didn't have any communication for a few months. In that time, I finished the book and they began their podcast.

I reached out to Brad to see if he would be attending the FinCon Conference centered around money and media. He responded that he was, and that's when he told me about the rise of their podcast. They were getting five-figure downloads per episode. He also informed me that he really enjoyed my book and wanted Jonathan to read it. We planned a meetup at the conference.

Inside the lobby, Jonathan, Brad, and I got together to finally meet in person. The conversation lasted a good forty-five minutes, and the topics ranged from family to business, travel and homeschooling. It was highly energized and personal, and I got a feeling for how great these two people were. As we finished, Jonathan asked for an advance copy of my book, which I sent that night.

After reading it on a flight to South Africa, Jonathan messaged me to tell me that he and Brad wanted to have me as a guest on the *Choose FI* podcast.

I was thrilled, and we set up the interview a few weeks before the book launched.

The response to the show was incredible and quite possibly gave the biggest boost to the book launch out of all of the interviews I did. Their reach—and the cohesiveness of our messages—made for a powerful conversation.

What Brad and Jonathan do differently is record a follow-up

episode talking about the previous interview, break down their take on it, and get feedback from their audience. It's a brilliant method that leads to added engagement and deeper content.

I didn't listen to the interview. Back then, I rarely listened to the episodes after I was interviewed. I hated listening to my voice, and nothing was more cringeworthy than listening to myself talk. I did listen to the follow-up. In that show, I learned a ton about myself. It was almost like an obituary, to be blunt. Listening to two people that you admire talk about you in front of a lot of people is an odd feeling.

The long-winded reason of why I wrote this story was because they described why they asked me to be on the show. Yes, they liked the book. Jonathan even said it was one of his favorites (they added it to their top three books on their website and gave away a copy weekly on their podcast), but that wasn't what won them over. I was really surprised to hear what did.

It was the fact that I kept eye contact with them during our entire conversation at FinCon. I was surprised to hear this because I didn't know I did. I always thought it was rude when I talked to others and they looked away during the conversation, so I make it a point not to do that. They also said that when they go to conferences, people tend to "look over their shoulders" to see if there is someone more important to talk to or introduce themselves to. They really liked that I didn't do that. When we were talking, they had my full attention. What is interesting is that I noticed that about them too.

Jonathan and Brad get tons of requests from potential guests to be on their show. But I didn't ask to be on the show; they asked me. And I'm not under any assumption that the book alone got me on the show. What they talked about in the post-interview opened my eyes to the intangibles that lead to success- intangibles that are rarely talked about in the online world.

Personal skills in conversations and relationships will always be a major aspect of success. Have you ever met that "online influencer" in person who had awful communication skills? The person who can make you laugh or think differently with something they write, but is a dud when you meet them? It puts a damper on their aura. It's become so easy that we often use social media as a shield. It's become something we can hide behind to avoid being human. But being human is what makes a person stand out.

So look people in the eyes during conversations. Don't look over their shoulder for someone else and make them feel unimportant. Be present. Be engaged. Be human.

It will open doors for you that won't happen without it.

Is It Wasted Time or a Hidden Secret?

"Secrets aren't secret. They're just hidden treasures, waiting to be explored."

— STEPHEN WHITE

Ken Carfagno is one of my closest friends. We met randomly at a conference in New York City years ago. I was wandering the hallways before the conference began when I overheard an interesting conversation. Not one to shy away, I slid in. Ken and I formed an immediate connection.

Each week after that conference, we got on the phone and began our first "mastermind." It was just the two of us, and those conversations often lasted two or three hours. We discussed our goals, dreams, and challenges, helping each other through our battles. The encouragement and support were invaluable to both of us as we began the journey on the next phase of our careers and lives.

Personal connection has always been at the core of how I like to roll. Even though it's not "scalable" in the business world, I thrive on having deep, meaningful conversations, even to the detriment of my work. I have been known to procrastinate on work in favor of personal conversations. (Note: for instance, this part of the book is being derailed by a text conversation with my friend, Josh Melton) Even though it can be a divergence, magical things happen during conversations. I started noticing such things outside of the relationships that were born.

It became clear that our businesses grew and thrived because of these conversations. Getting on these calls to connect—and with no expectations—led to a greater trust between us. We were able to cut through all the internet mumbo jumbo and see how we might help each other. I was able to figure out ways to connect them to people in my network and at times coach them through difficult situations. Each of these conversations made me better at all the things I love to do, which led to more and more business.

Ken is a former engineer. His brain works much differently than mine. He is the structured, regimented planner who likes everything in place with a reason for it all. I couldn't be more different. His organized, problem-solving mind offers him plenty of amazing advantages, but a few years ago he was stuck. Where I would spend my days in various, unplanned conversations, he was knocking out his to-do list like there was no tomorrow. As productive as he was, he wasn't seeing much progress in growing his business teaching cleaners how to run a profitable cleaning business.

I encouraged him to get on more calls, build those relationships, and allow those conversations to grow organically. You can't understand the magic of this until you do it consistently.

Ken pushed back because he thought it would be time wasted because it would take away from the task work he needed to do.

One Friday, he messaged me because he was frustrated with himself. That day, his to-do list had been blown up and taken completely off course. None of the things he planned got done as he was wrapped up in phone calls all day. Three conversations took up the better part of his day, and the irritation in his usually calm voice was evident.

As an afterthought, he mentioned that one of those calls became a new client, another started as a casual conversation that became an unexpected cleaning client, and the third helped a friend solve a major issue that led to a breakthrough in his business. To my surprise and subsequent laughter, he repeated how unproductive his day was.

"You should hope every day is that unproductive," I quipped.

"What do you mean?" Ken responded.

"All of your to-do lists," I asked. "What is the goal of them?"

His engineering brain caught up at breakneck speed. I could hear him put all the pieces together without a sound from five hundred miles away.

"That they lead to exactly what happened today," Ken said. "Except this happened much faster and in a way that was really fun to do. For the first time, I see what you've been saying. This wasn't wasted time at all. I actually think it's the hidden secret."

And that mastermind that we started on a whim, just the two of us? That turned into our *Total Life Freedom Mastermind*, which has been a six-figure business and the pivot that we made from photography, which gave us a deeper level of freedom than we've ever had before. And Ken Carfagno is one of the original members.

Are personal conversations unscalable wasted time for you or your hidden secret?

Psychic Compensation

"There is compensation in all things." —ANNA LEONOWENS

I'm not sure where you are on this journey. Wherever you are, know that everyone is struggling with something. You can be on top of the world career-wise but disconnected emotionally from your family. You can have great relationships but suffer great physical or emotional pain. You can be at the beginning of a new or different career and feel completely lost and overwhelmed.

Do you remember when I went to "shoot the pope?" That was one of the first of many new career transitions. Each time there were periods of worry, uncertainty, and doubt I had to fight through to make it to the other side.

While I was busy trying to shoot the pope, I was also a waiter at The Spare Rib, taking classes at Nassau Community College, and working in a photo printing store. I would process film, take customer orders, and replenish the machines. It was there where I caught a lucky break. I made it clear to anyone who was interested that my dream was to be a sports photographer. As crappy as that photo lab job was, one perk was that I could print my own pictures when the boss wasn't around.

One afternoon, I was printing my portfolio when a customer named Fred Klein entered the store. Klein was a highly respected attorney in our area, and I went to high school with his son Alex. Klein curiously asked what I was working on, and I told him about my dream. He casually mentioned how he was friends with Shelly Finkel, Mike Tyson's manager. Klein said that Finkel had ties to *Sports Illustrated*, which was the dream job for any sports photographer. With a simple gesture, he offered to connect the two of us. Days later, I was on the phone talking to one of the biggest boxing promoters in the world and the manager for "the baddest man on the planet."

Karma set in deeper when, during that conversation, we realized that Finkel and my dad went to the same school—Brooklyn Tech—a few years apart. At the end of the call, he told me that he would take my portfolio to *Sports Illustrated* to see if there was a future there.

I was stunned. I was a little more than a year into trying this—with no luck so far—and my portfolio would be inside the doors of the biggest sports magazine in the world.

I waited impatiently to hear a response. A few weeks later, Klein entered the store, portfolio in hand, to deliver the bad news.

"They said you show promise," he told me, "but as of now, you are just a beginner."

He could see the disappointment in my face. I was back to square one. No paid work. No access. And the only connection I had just rejected me. I doubted out loud if I had what it took to make it. Two weeks later, Klein returned to the store. After another conversation about my stalled career, he walked toward the exit. I got his attention before he left.

"You know, all of my classmates in high school and college, they all graduated and have careers started. I'm six years out, and I'm stuck in a dead-end job," I complained. "*I am such a loser for working here*."

Klein stopped at the door, making a comment before walking out.

"You are not a loser for working here," he said, "but if you are still working here in five years, you *are* a loser."

I quit the job at Prestige Photo a few weeks later to go full force on my career. I had to take action in the present to not be that loser in the future. I didn't see Klein again after that so I didn't get to tell him that five years later, I was on the sidelines in the New Orleans Superdome photographing the Super Bowl in the middle of my dream career.

Last year, I realized that not only did I never get to thank Klein, but he had no idea the impact his words had on me. Just like Funzi, he came into my world in a flash, uttered words that changed my life, and was gone just as quick. So I needed to track him down. I searched online with no luck. I then remembered that I was connected to his son online. I reached out to tell Alex the impact his father had on me, and he gave me his dad's phone number.

I called and recognized the voice immediately. Although he was relaxing on the beach in Key West as opposed to the courts in New York, that same energy and fire was there. I filled him in on all that had happened since we connected and how it never would have happened without his belief and his declaration. Being willing to put himself out there and use his network to help a kid like me made a big impression, and his "loser" comment sprang me into action.

During our conversation, we bonded because we both saw that we had very similar school experiences. He graduated from the same high school I did, exactly thirty years earlier. And after Klein earned an impressive SAT score, his guidance counselor told him that it must have been a mistake because he couldn't possibly score that high. He told me that the doubts others had in his abilities fueled his success. After I told him my very similar guidance counselor story, he declared us to be soul mates.

He told me what his mother taught him at a young age: it's always better to give than receive. And it always comes around. Twenty-four years later, I had the privilege to thank him for what he did for me.

"You have given *me* something today," Mr. Klein informed me. "It's compensation, but not the usual way people look at compensation. People are always looking for monetary compensation. What you have given to me is psychic compensation."

When you do good for people—when you help without expectation and connect with people for the right reasons—you receive psychic compensation, meaning you will be rewarded even if you do not know it. You continue living your life unaware that others appreciate you. They say good things about you. They talk positively about you when you aren't around. You don't hear it, but trust that it's out there and is making your life better. Later on—maybe even twenty-four years later—you get a thank-you that proves that psychic compensation is real, and it may be the most powerful compensation you'll ever receive from a life well-lived.

The Value of Connection

Character and Curiosity are the foundational parts of *The Wealth of Connection*. Connection and Collaboration are the relational parts. Creation is the final piece- it's the exponential part that will lead to the massive success that comes from doing the foundational and relational parts.

They are all incredibly important. Naming the most valuable one is like trying to name your favorite child. Each one is equally as valuable in its own unique way. Without solid character and curiosity, it's impossible to develop solid connections. Well, it's impossible to develop connections with people who also have character and curiosity. You will develop connections with people who don't have those things. Yet to go deeper, we need to learn to read the room. It only gets better when you learn how to name names, remember names, and give credit. We can get so wrapped up in our own lives, our own selfish goals, that we don't learn to simply pay attention.

When you consistently keep in touch by valuing The Hour of Giving, you come to not only enjoy connecting the unconnected, but you see the massive value that comes from it for you and for the members of your network. By focusing on this more, you begin to see who your two-minute friends are as well as your two-day friends. It could be an important exercise that allows you to see- and go- where you are celebrated and notice where you are simply tolerated.

And instead of keeping score and looking for credit, you might realize that psychic compensation may be the most rewarding compensation of them all.

Part 4

COLLABORATION

Value Growth More Than Grind

Do You Compete or Collaborate?

"Some people make things happen, some people watch what happens and some people ask, "what happened?" — DAVID LEE ROTH

Racing upstairs to my bedroom, it was a rare night of me wanting to go to bed early. Waiting upstairs was my trusty Walkman and the cassette tape of Van Halen, the first album by the rock and roll icons. They were the biggest rock band in the world in 1984 (their new single Jump was the number one song in the United States for six weeks). Having just entered my teenage years, I was unfamiliar with their early music.

My friend Rich Samuels and I were often in detention together after school, and music was the only thing we talked about. It was in detention where he handed me a cassette tape of Van Halen's debut album.

"You have to listen to this," he marveled. "I've never heard anything like it."

That evening, I said goodnight to my parents early and rushed upstairs. Under the covers, I put my headphones on, pressed play on my knockoff tape player, (I couldn't afford a real Walkman) and proceeded to listen in awe. Rich was spot on. I'd never heard anything like this before.

The combination of the monster guitar riffs of Eddie Van Halen and the over the top vocals from David Lee Roth entranced me from the start. Eddie Van Halen then launched into "Eruption," a nearly two minute guitar solo that is widely considered the best guitar solo of all time. I was now hopelessly hooked. I rewinded and played that tape so often that it eventually snapped.

By 1984, Van Halen appeared larger than life. In their humble beginnings, that would never have been imagined.

The Van Halen brothers- Eddie and drummer Alex- were immersed in the world of music from the start. Their father Jan was a professional clarinetist, saxophonist, and pianist. Once Eddie discovered the guitar and Alex began playing drums, their lives revolved around learning and practicing. When they eventually formed a band, their presence was heavy on the music, but nearly void of any stage presence. The brothers and their bandmates barely moved on stage while wearing their standard outfit of jeans and t-shirts. It was all about the music.

For eventual bandmate David Lee Roth, it couldn't have been more different. Roth possessed boundless energy as a child. His parents labeled his wild antics at home as "The Monkey Hour," where he would perform nightly for the family. Roth managed to turn Monkey Hour into a lucrative and prosperous career. For Roth, it was a relentless amount of energy, style, and flash that got himself noticed and his name out there.

Both the Van Halen brothers and David Lee Roth lived in Pasadena, California and eventually became competitors in different bands. As they grew in the ranks, they certainly knew of each other and were aware of what their competition was up to. Roth, with his flashy stage presence, admired the talent of Van Halen while trying to outdo them. The Van Halen brothers couldn't stand David Lee Roth.

Roth, sensing an opportunity to blend his style with their substance, auditioned for the band, and was promptly rejected. His singing was subpar and his stage presence was too much. After another failed audition, Roth eventually bartered his way into the band. Van Halen (then named Mammoth) was low on cash and Roth owned a fabulous PA system. Roth gave them the system in exchange for him getting the lead singer gig. It was one of the greatest trades in history.

Competitors, who weren't going far on their own, became collaborators. Roth now had the talent around him to fuel the marketing, business, and publicity to create a world class band. Van Halen had the push to get out of the musically advanced yet visually boring backyard shows they had been playing around Pasadena. Roth convinced his new bandmates to lose the jeans and t-shirts and bring more flash to their shows. Instead of standing perfectly still like he used to, Eddie Van Halen developed a highly energized presence of jumping off of risers, displaying a blitzkrieg of energy while doing it all with a huge smile on his face.

Van Halen persuaded David Lee Roth to level up his vocal range. While Roth appeared to be nothing but a flamboyant party animal, behind the scenes he was relentlessly honing his craft while remaining incredibly coachable.

As competitors, their reach was limited and their ceiling for growth was stunted. According to Greg Renoff, the author of *Van Halen Rising*, a major label record executive attempted to persuade the band by telling them that he would work with the band if they fired Roth. This executive said that Roth was holding them back. Others close to the band pushed for that as well. But Eddie Van Halen knew differently.

"We need him," Van Halen declared.

Eddie Van Halen understood the power of collaboration. He appreciated what Roth brought to the band and he was loyal enough to not throw him away for quick success. According to music critic Stephen Thomas Ealewine, Van Halen's eventual first album set the template for how rock and roll sounded for the next decade or more.

Collaboration requires that we work in tandem, using teamwork, empathy, and understanding beyond our own wants and needs. It naturally helps build stronger relationships because our mission is to achieve a collective goal. It takes us away from the winner-takes-all, me-first mentality that accompanies competition. And possibly most important, it helps us build and nurture relationships in a healthy, mutually beneficial way. Helpful people want to help helpful people.

Through these collaborative efforts, others get to see how our strengths might help them or those they know. What comes from great collaboration is an even greater network. And if you are going to build the life that opens doors for you and those around you, you must build your powerful network.

Why We Need a Powerful Network

"Instead of better glasses, your network gives you better eyes."

— RONALD BURT

I'm guessing that you aren't a guitar virtuoso or a high profile, attention seeking rock singer. You might be thinking- that's cool for them. But what if you don't have world class musical talent? What if you're not even sure what you want to do with your life at the moment but you know you need to have better connections and a stronger network?

I have been faced with this question a number of times myself. I had an idea of what I wanted but I had no idea how to get there and I had nobody to help me. Feeling stuck, alone, and unsure, I'd often feel resentful and even jealous of others. I had enough experience to see that there was a pattern here. I eventually learned to break the pattern by doing just one thing.

I restarted The Hour of Giving. That's it. I needed to take the focus off of myself. It literally was making me depressed. Without fail, each time The Hour of Giving started, my mood changed. Connections restarted in an instant. I didn't wait for someone to initiate- I had to do it. Within days, old relationships reemerged and new ones blossomed. Why did I stop doing this?

Immediately, the resurgence of my network felt valuable. I'd kick myself for not being consistent because new opportunities were arriving after just weeks of doing so. How many great things would be available if I didn't stop? But there's no room for beating ourselves up about it. We just need to continue being better than yesterday. We need to reenforce the idea that our generous goals need to go on top of selfish goals.

Everything we want for ourselves we need to do for others first. There is no better way to earn trust than to support others. What is so intriguing about this is that the people who have generous goals wind up with financial and career success at a much higher level than those who actually focus just on themselves. It sounds counterintuitive but reciprocity is a scientifically proven fact.

When your goals focus on generosity, other generous people will begin to trust you. Generous people don't enjoy being around selfish people in case you haven't noticed. They prefer to surround themselves with givers while simultaneously repelling the selfish. Have you heard the phrase "the rich get richer and the poor get poorer"? It might not be as nefarious as it's often made out to be. The generous develop a network of people around them that understand this. And as they do this, they develop a powerful network that ironically yields more sales, better prospects, deeper relationships, better health, and more happiness— everything they want out of life.

Earlier I said that nobody cares about your goals. Now I will say, it's not that *nobody* cares. You probably have a few people in your life that do.

But if you don't have people connecting you to the people you want to be around— people around you promoting you and sharing your work— your network is too weak. There are not enough people in your world opening doors for you. There are too few people telling others about you. There are not enough peers to brainstorm with, influencers to elevate you, and clients to invest in you.

This is why building a powerful network is the hidden advantage of just about everyone who is doing what you want to do and achieving what you want to achieve— even beyond your wildest dreams. Have you ever heard the phrase "you don't know what you don't know"? What isn't heard often is that you don't know *whom* you don't know.

Notice that I didn't say you need a huge network. I said a powerful one. A network of people you care about and who care about you. Not only do most people have a weak network, but they also build their network selfishly, which destroys the little network they do have.

It's Going to Take a Year

"Move quick, but don't hurry."— JOHN WOODEN

When we travel with our kids, we hear the same question over and over: "How long until we're there?" Elizabeth or I would explain the distance, and where we were traveling to, but it was rarely good enough. We'd stop for lunch, and then the time would change and they would get confused or frustrated.

So, in our own frustration, we changed the answer. We started saying twenty minutes. Every. Single. Time. Now, we weren't totally lying to them. We were going to be somewhere in twenty minutes. Eventually, when one of the kids asked, one of their brothers would blurt out, "Twenty minutes!"

Mission accomplished.

I get the same question here. How long does it take to build a powerful network? My answer is always the same. It's going to take a year. Now, in reality, that isn't true either. A year is far too little and sometimes more than you need. It's rarely a year, just like we were never twenty minutes from Grandma's house. But a year gives you patience, and it gives you persistence. It's far enough away that you don't become desperate, but soon enough that you can't get complacent. If you build your network consistently for a year without wanting anything back, magical things happen. It affords you the opportunity to connect in a way that feels different then reaching out when you need something. It's always a year away. And it will always be better one year from now.

I'll refer back to The Hour of Giving once again. Jennifer was an executive with Giant Eagle, a supermarket powerhouse in Pennsylvania and Ohio. Jennifer had hired our company to work on many of their events- which were lucrative gigs. Eventually, Jennifer was offered a position at a different company and moved on from Giant Eagle.

We loved working with her, and Elizabeth and I were disappointed that our working relationship had ended. If we took the "me first" approach, it would have been easy to lose touch and dismiss Jennifer as someone not necessary to keep in touch with. But with The Hour of Giving, checking in on her and seeing how she was doing was a part of the wealth of connection.

I reached out several months later to see how she was enjoying her job. It turned out that she wasn't enjoying it at all. In fact, she was getting ready to leave and do what she had always wanted to do- start her own business.

"I am so grateful that you reached out," she followed. "I need to hire you to help get this started!"

That created instant, well paying income. I have dozens upon dozens of stories of work, media, podcast interviews, and referrals coming in simply from reconnecting with no expectations during The Hour of Giving. Often, it's years in the making before something unexpected happens.

If you give yourself a year head start, you can accomplish almost anything. There is nothing quite like having patience, persistence, and a calm vision. But why do so many people fail to build a powerful network for themselves? Do they not see the importance of a vibrant network that will give them access to the things they desire? Many do, and amazingly, too many don't. But the ones who do often do it the wrong way. They try to build it based only on what they want or need, an approach usually born of selfishness or desperation—or both. No matter the combination, it's not a sustainable way to build a powerful network. If your vision takes place over the next year, you'll have a plan going forward.

Aside from your integrity, there is nothing more important in business than the power of your network. Some will argue that your vision, your product, or your style is the most important. I would vehemently disagree with that assessment. We can be coerced into thinking that all the bells and whistles that are pitched and sold to us are essential to building a thriving venture. Yet nothing is more important than the power of a network as a nucleus around everything you are building now and into the future.

A powerful network unlocks doors. It presents opportunities that never would have been made available through hard work alone. Such a network gives us the opportunity to bring people together who normally don't have the opportunity to meet. Our personal connections make that happen. It's easy to downplay the power of our own network as well as the connections within them. It's common to focus on doing the work that needs to get done today while ignoring the compound importance of connecting with your network on a daily basis.

It's important to understand that nobody else in the world has a network of connections like you do. It might be smaller than you like. It might not be as strong as you want. But you have a network that is as unique as a snowflake. The problem is that we consistently undervalue those connections. We don't realize the vast power that lies within them. We don't think about how inside that network is the key to success for us and those who surround us.

Surround Yourself with People Smarter than You

"If you are dumb, surround yourself with smart people. If you are smart, surround yourself with smart people who will disagree with you."

— AARON SORKIN

Never underestimate your past while learning the lessons for your future. When I say your past, I specifically mean stories that have nothing to do with what you are working on today. Experiences that seem to have no correlation to your current business or venture. Drawing from these lessons brings your message the uniqueness that nobody else has experienced and is one of the edges that you— and only you— possess. So when you read the upcoming story, understand that this practice is what allowed me to build a powerful network and gain all the value that comes from that.

Elizabeth and I were together right out of college for our first full-time photojournalist positions. The jobs were at a newspaper in Evansville, Indiana, a place I knew little about aside from the fact that the newspaper was renowned for its world-class photography staff. Oh, and former New York Yankee Don Mattingly was from there. I knew nothing else, yet there we were, at a newspaper where photography was taken seriously— a far cry from the majority of newspapers that viewed the photo department as second-class citizens next to the writers.

Bruce Baumann was the reason why. Baumann was the quintessential old-school newspaper personality. Energetic, gruff, and at times outrageous, Baumann became the managing editor of his hometown paper to cap off his career after a lifetime of achievements building photographic newspaper forces from Pittsburgh to Monterey, along with leading the premier photo haven for decades: *National Geographic*. When Baumann returned to Evansville to take over, his credentials and experience were unmatched, and he was determined to use the power of photography to make the paper stand out. By doing so, he ushered in a new era that turned the Evansville photo department into a tour de force of local, national, and international award winners.

In our third year at the paper, the staff once again took the majority of the awards at the yearly state journalism conference, leading one of the staffers from the competing *Indianapolis Star* to pull me aside.

"What is in the water down there?" he asked. "How does a staff of only six people win nearly every award?"

There wasn't anything in the water. It was Baumann. It didn't matter what city he was in. It didn't matter the size of the newspaper. If he was in charge, the staff around him would be of the highest caliber. It would be respected by the rest of the newsroom. And it would stand out above the rest. Was Baumann always nice? Not a chance. Others in the newsroom despised him. Why? Because he had high standards for photography, which took power away from the other departments.

In one instance, a highly connected reporter was working on a long-term project. It was an incredible story but this reporter didn't connect with the photo staff throughout the process. One afternoon, Elizabeth received a photo request form for this particular story (these forms were changed from assignments to requests because, well, reporters no longer gave photographers assignments. They requested them.) Confused as to why she was being asked to shoot a last-minute photo of a story that obviously needed more time, Elizabeth showed it to Baumann. He summoned the reporter to his office.

"How long did you work on this story?"

"I've been working hard on this for three months," the reporter proudly responded.

"Wonderful," he countered. "Elizabeth now has three months to document this before we publish."

That reporter walked out of his office angry, but Elizabeth took that photo request and created a stunning visual story of a family struggling with their little girl's autism. She spent three months with them, to the point where she was called family. And the final result was a wonderfully written story with outstanding visual images that not only won all of the awards, it impacted our community.

So, while that reporter left in a huff, Baumann's support for his staff is what made the photographers Baumann hired take so much pride in their work. I asked him, in the middle of the stunning run of success in Evansville, how he was able to create such an amazing staff at every paper.

"Always surround yourself with people who are smarter than you," he responded confidently. "No amount of intelligence will make you look better in this environment than being around and working with intelligent people."

Baumann knew that if he brought in the right people, everything else would fall into place if he had high standards.

Who we surround ourselves with has more to do with the success of our careers and our lives than we are led to believe.

Success by Association

"Trust is earned, respect is given, and loyalty is demonstrated. Betrayal of any one of those is to lose all three." —ZIAD K. ABDELNOUR

I was sixteen years old when I nervously picked up the phone in my parents' bedroom. On the other end of the line was this girl I met the day before. After my friends and I narrowly escaped the police (a not-so-uncommon encounter), we met up with this girl and her group of friends to lay low and avoid being found. Deep down, I knew I shouldn't be there. I was far from the ringleader. When I wasn't hanging out with the wild crowd, I was home watching professional wrestling or some game on television. I wasn't a bad kid nor did I crave mayhem. But there was just something about the recklessness and carefree way these guys went about life that I found attractive.

So there I was, sitting in the dirt surrounded by a dozen teenagers drinking warm beer on an ever-warmer night, laughing nervously about the trouble we just avoided. I, however, was more focused on the girl sitting across from me. She had the right combination of girl-next-door looks and rebellious attitude that made me get over my fear long enough to strike up a conversation. Next thing I knew, I had her phone number.

The next day, my heart pounded as her phone rang. She answered curtly, putting me on edge from the start. The conversation loosened up with a few laughs as we reminisced about what took place the night before. I then made the critical mistake of asking what her plans were for the summer.

"Plans?" she responded while pausing to take a sip of something. "Don't tell me you're the type of person that makes *plans*."

"Oh, of course not," I said with my fake, cool, sixteen-year-old demeanor. "I don't make plans!"

Even though I did. Otherwise, I wouldn't have asked that question. I can't pinpoint the exact moment, but soon after I kept hearing the phrase "guilt by association." For the next few years, as my friendships became more about the trouble we got into and less about the things we would accomplish, guilt by association took shape in every area of my life. Even if I didn't cause trouble, I became labeled by hanging out with those who did.

This continued until the night when someone who had been a close friend had an interesting encounter in front of a local market late one evening. Even though he was troubled throughout school, his penchant for drug use, theft, and overall lawlessness went up a few levels after graduation. One evening, he was low on cash as well as his stash. He had no money to buy drugs. So he waited in the dark outside this store until a potential victim walked past.

In an instant, he jumped out to rob this woman, grabbing her purse in a struggle and ran away.

In most situations, that would be the end of the story. But less than an hour later, the police were at his home putting him in handcuffs and taking him to jail.

Of all people to rob, he happened to rob a police sketch artist. She went right to the station, drew up the perfect picture of her assailant, and they immediately knew his face. An extensive stay in jail followed.

I caused my own problems, but they were compounded exponentially by the company I kept.

Of course, there is an entirely different side of it. My former classmates— the ones I chose not to hang out with— all seemed to be starting great careers. They were recommended by one another's parents and were brought in for internships, apprentices, and well-paying positions. They were known in the community for their hard work, helpfulness, and good attitudes. And as they worked together to get better, they all seemed to wind up in great spots. Because they were so well-respected, other business owners asked if there was anyone else in their crowd looking for work. Mark, a friend of mine who straddled the line between spending time with us and with them, was one of them.

I ran into him at the local 7-Eleven shortly after I was arrested for stealing. I was scraping by, working a minimum-wage job while trying to pay my new legal bills. We chatted briefly before he had to run. He was on his way to work for a television station in New York City, working in the sports department with the broadcasters. I was floored and quite honestly, jealous. Very jealous. It was a job I would have loved to have had I even known it was a job.

"How'd you get that gig?" I asked, trying not to sound too jealous.

"Oh, remember Adam?" he said. "His dad runs the station. We were all hanging out at their house for a cookout a few months ago, and I was talking about how much I love sports. Apparently, he heard me say that and he asked around. The next thing I know, I had a job interview! Sorry, Vin, I need to run to work. Great seeing you!" he said in a hurry.

I stood there holding my Slurpee as he drove away. My friends are getting arrested. His friends are getting him his dream job. I lived in the world of "Guilt by Association." They lived in the world of "Success by Association."

Which are you going to choose?

The Feedback Loop

"Your competition is not other people but the time you kill, the ill will you create, the knowledge you neglect to learn, the connections you fail to build, the health you sacrifice along the path, your inability to generate ideas, the people around you who don't support and love your efforts, and whatever god you curse for your bad luck." — JAMES ALTUCHER

One of the key aspects of successful collaboration is how well feedback is handled. The difference between someone who seeks and embraces feedback and those who avoid or get defensive with feedback is often the difference between someone who builds a powerful, trusting and collaborative network and someone who winds up working alone, frustrated, and with a revolving door of new connections who never develop into collaborative relationships.

And people who run at the highest levels are open to always learning and collaborating from people they trust. They know that, as great as they are, it takes a team to make them perform at world-class levels.

And how we accept, acknowledge, and seek out feedback is a key component in all of this. Being unable to accept feedback is a sign of someone who is either too proud, too insecure, or too arrogant to realize that they will never achieve the levels they aspire to. Have you ever been told that you are defensive? Did you get defensive when they said that? *Long pause required here*. Feedback is always there to help you improve. Now, what you do with that feedback is up to you, but your harshest critics might be offering you your most valuable feedback.

Instead of getting offended by it, imagine how difficult it is for someone who cares about you to actually give that feedback. Unless it's done in an unhealthy way (while acknowledging that they *still* might have a point), we should draw those people closer to us because they are willing to put their necks on the line to give you criticism you find difficult to hear. The ones who are willing to lose a friendship to tell you the truth are way more valuable than those who tell you what you want to hear because they fear confrontation.

We now live in a culture where feedback is shunned and shamed. If someone offers feedback, they are labeled as haters. So we gravitate toward the people who praise us, no matter how little we have earned that praise. Look no further than politics on this one. It's called confirmation bias. We search for people and information that supports how we feel or how we believe. People on the "other side" are ignored, made fun of, or dismissed flippantly.

When you never think you're wrong, you find no reason to improve. You dismiss the feelings of others who love you, want to see you do better, and might actually get hurt by your choices. But in the world of collaboration, the ability to gratefully receive feedback is essential to your growth and that of your network.

The key— as we have talked about early and often— is trust. If you don't trust someone, there is a high chance that you won't trust their feedback. Conversely, if you haven't built up trust with a person, group, or organization, it's going to be an uphill battle to get them to trust you.

All Apologies

"A sincere apology is the super glue of life. It can repair just about anything."

— LYNN JOHNSTON

When I was a kid, *Happy Days* was one of the most popular shows on television. Based in Wisconsin, it was set in the 1950s and 1960s and was based on the high school and college years of a group of kids in post-World-War-II America, hanging out at Al's Diner. The most memorable character was Arthur Fonzarelli, known as "The Fonz." His character— leather jacket on the outside, exuding coolness on the inside, and a magnet for the girls— made him the star of the show. He had a tough demeanor that scared off troublemakers, yet he was the one the kids came to for advice, resolve a conflict, or bring others together.

Despite all this adoration, The Fonz also had a weak spot. Whether it was because of extreme confidence or some other factor, The Fonz had trouble saying one single word. In fact, every time he tried to say that word, he'd get tongue-tied and stutter. The word just couldn't escape his mouth. On the rare occasion he attempted to utter this word, it came out like this: "I was wroo...I was wrrrrrrr...I was wwwwrruuuoo..."

The Fonz simply could not say he was wrong.

Neither can many of us. I've been no different. Saying that I'm wrong has been one of the hardest words for me to utter. And when I do, it's with blood running down my lip from biting it so hard while uttering that painful word.

Why? No one around me did either.

"I might not be right, but I'm never wrong," was a line my grandmother said throughout my childhood. Everyone always laughed because it was Grandma. But I never liked it. I didn't like what it meant and saw those seeds planting so many of my childhood struggles. We threw around apologies like we threw around manhole covers. An apology was a rare occurrence, and when it was done, it was usually said as, "I'm *sorrrrry*," in an arrogant, sarcastic, or dismissive way just to get the conversation finished.

But there are other ways to apologize incorrectly.

"I'm sorry that you feel that way," I said to a coworker after he told me that something I did made him feel undervalued.

"Was that supposed to be an apology?" he asked flippantly.

"Well, yeah, I guess so," I muttered, not sure what I really meant by it. It was just something I, and so many others, say.

"*You* are sorry that *I* feel that way?" he responded, stressing the words *you* and *I*. "What a lame apology! So you didn't do anything wrong here— you're just sorry for the way I feel?"

I was taken aback. He was spot on. I'm sorry that he feels a certain way. I get to use the word sorry while never apologizing for anything. It's an empty and condescending "apology."

I carried these conversational flaws into my marriage. I perceived apologies as a sign of weakness. If I apologized, it meant I had a shortcoming, a deficiency. I was the one who gave in and was defeated. I viewed it as a competition I wasn't going to lose. When you have this type of mindset, you tend to get good at arguing simply because you often find yourself on the defensive. Not admitting you are wrong can become an unfortunate strength because the better you get at it, the more you win arguments you weren't right about.

I saw what this did to Elizabeth. She would back down because she didn't want to fight, and that would give me the opportunity to go in for the win. The more I deflected from my responsibilities and focused on trivial points I could bend in my favor, the more I wore her down. So disagreement after disagreement, I'd win.

It didn't feel like much of a victory because Elizabeth would get increasingly frustrated with me. She didn't feel heard or appreciated. She hesitated to bring things up because she didn't want another courtroom battle.

On those rare occasions where, unlike The Fonz, I got an apology out, Elizabeth was so much more appreciative. We would reestablish conversation, and she would open up about things she didn't feel comfortable saying when I was always "right." There was a relief on her face just hearing me say those words. Suddenly, it didn't matter if I was right or wrong. What I thought would make me weak actually made her feel more loved, which then allowed me to be more vulnerable with my apologies because I didn't feel that sense of weakness. She seemed grateful, which is a much better reaction than being afraid or apprehensive.

An apology, if done without outside pressure, isn't a sign of weakness. It's a generous act that shows humility and appreciation, which are both attractive traits. It validates, respects, and edifies the other person. And they usually wind up forgiving you much quicker from a sincere apology than they ever will by you always having to be right. I realize now that my grandmother would have done a much better job if she just cut off the second part of her statement.

"I might not be right," she could have said, and left it at that.

Put People Over

"The next level for all of us is owning the fact that if we don't live for others, then there's victory for none of us." — BRENDON BURCHARD

While working for World Wrestling Entertainment, I learned phrases and thought processes I had never heard before. They were industry-specific, which made it both confusing and fascinating to figure out. It was usually my more experienced coworkers who would get me caught up in the lingo. In the wild world of professional wrestling, there were storylines everywhere I looked. We had the champion, the contenders, and the up-and-comers. We also had the good guys and the bad guys. The good guys were called "baby faces" and the bad guys were called "heels." There were times that the heels turned into baby faces and baby faces flipped and turned heel. It was always a wide array of moving parts because, in a world like that, you can't have the same thing happening over and over again. You need surprising drama and story lines to keep the audience on their toes, unsure what is coming next. As soon as you become predictable, you are done.

But it's difficult to manage that when you have a hierarchy of wrestlers who are widely known and respected by the crowd because they always brought in the audience and consistently brought in the energy. Yet you can't stick with the same act forever. You need them to shift around and have the good guys lose or turn heel and stun the crowd— despite the intense loyalty fans developed with certain wrestlers.

Because they were so respected, it was hard for the up-and-comers to get the fans' approval. So there is a phrase in that world called "putting someone over." It means that established wrestlers who have earned the trust and adulation of their fan base have an obligation to help elevate others. How do you elevate those who are on the way up? It's a mix of art and science, but they figure out when the time is right to elevate someone from the rank-and-file to elite status and fan favorite. At a certain point, one of those up-and-comers is ready to become champion. But it takes one of the elites to get them there.

That is putting someone over.

The champion, in essence, agrees to let one of the up-and-comers defeat him and win over the crowd. When the new guy beats the champion, it earns the respect of the crowd, and they no longer look at the new guy as someone who hasn't earned their stripes. They look at them as someone who beat the best. I got a backstage pass to see this happen. It's amazing how so many of these little things that seem unrelatable are actually very relatable to our own lives. I've had many times in my life where people have put me over. People who went out of their way— when they didn't need to— to use their influence and allow me to gain a higher status, whether it was within an organization or for another person.

I think of Jim Jorden, who gave me my first press pass at Lambeau Field, which launched my career. I think of Bruce Baumann, who hired Elizabeth and me and put us on one of the best photo staffs in the country. I think of Larry Hagner, who gave me my first opportunity to lead a mastermind within his *Dad Edge Alliance*, which planted the seeds for everything we are doing with the *Total Life Freedom Mastermind Community*.

I have hundreds of examples of people who have done that for me, and how they did not need to do it. At least for me they didn't. So now, for me, it is a mission of mine to put people over that I trust and to use my network, platform, and influence to get them from where they are to where they want to be. We live in such a me-me-me-oriented society that we are often competing rather than collaborating. And not just collaborating but supporting one another. And not just supporting successful people, but supporting people that you know need the help you have the ability to give.

It's important to know that you can't do this for everybody. If you don't know them, or they haven't earned the trust, then you can't put them over. These wrestlers didn't just put these kids over. They got to see their work ethic and integrity. When the up-and-comers earned the right and when the champions felt comfortable, they brought the new guys into the spotlight. Because nothing is worse than putting someone over who hasn't earned it.

So as you build your network, your platform, and your influence, never forget to put the people over who are in your life once they have earned it and need a boost. It makes the people around you better, and it makes your world stronger. And it gives you the foundation to build new worlds around it.

Bring Worlds Together

"Don't limit yourself to just connecting with people in your specific field."

— JEN HANSARD

A key to expanding your reach and influence into different "worlds" is your ability to bring those worlds together. As you have been generous, curious, and connected— especially with an expanded view of venturing into different worlds— you have the ability for exponential growth of your business and your ability to bring people together. Most people stay in their own lanes. They don't venture out to try new things or meet new people. It's scary and intimidating. So they stick with what they know.

It's like a former newspaper colleague said to me while we were traveling for an assignment. When we'd go to new places, I always wanted to try local restaurants and dishes. But he would only eat at McDonald's. When I asked why he always got the same food at the same place, his answer was typical.

"I know what I'm going to get when I go to McDonald's," he said with certainty.

And that is why most people do a poor job in connecting and collaborating— and why you have an amazing advantage if you do this. I suggest taking the DISC profile (a personality assessment tool) if you haven't already. DISC stands for the four main personality profiles: D (Dominant), I (Influence), S (Steadiness) and C (Conscientious). As you might tell by the names, S (Steadiness) doesn't like change. Interestingly enough, the S personality makes up the majority of the population. So, the majority of the population is resistant to change. They go to McDonald's because they know what they will get, they go to the same vacation spots every year, and they stay in jobs for decades longer than they want to because the pain they don't know seems worse than the pain they do know.

Alas, the success they don't know is also eluding them. After all, it's the ones willing to step out of their comfort zone that are brave enough to venture into a new world. They are willing to face rejection in order to form new connections and subsequently use that skill and generosity to bring others together.

Why people don't do this more baffles me. If they realized the power and influence they have among the people who trust them, they would see how unstoppable they could be. Bringing those worlds together goes back to what we talked about with Connect the Unconnected. When you can expand your circle into different worlds, this becomes magical.

You develop the trust within different communities and can see what others need and who they need to meet. That's when you can bring them together. You get to fill the gaps in your network and use your connections to make all of their lives better. I just want to know why this wasn't taught in school.

How hard is it to do, really? You pay attention to your friends' struggles. By noticing what others don't, you develop a superpower that makes you a unique linchpin in the lives of so many around you. You get to be the one who lifts up those in your circle, and you get to do it within your trusted network, which makes your entire network stronger.

So who benefits when you make your network stronger? Obviously, those you connect. You've strengthened their connections and have helped solve their most pressing issues. Who else benefits? Why, you of course! Because even though you don't "get" anything out of it, you get to experience the Helper's High and gain a stronger network since multiple people have gotten stronger themselves. When you lift up your network, you rise too. Your success by association factor gets stronger. And when you are at that conference later on and people are asked how they know each other, they point at you. Yet another quality connection comes into your powerful network.

This is what happens when you focus on bringing worlds together.

Who Do You Know That I Should Know?

"Producing is nothing more than bringing all the elements together, connecting people." — BRIAN JAMES

Once you have built trust inside a relationship, there is a question you might want to get into the habit of asking.

Who do you know that I should know?

I learned this question from John Maxwell, the author of more than seventy books, including *How Successful People Think*, *Failing Forward*, and the *15 Invaluable Laws of Growth*. Maxwell teaches that asking questions is the best way to be a leader, and this is one of the questions he teaches us to ask. This question, he has learned, can open some major doors you might never get access to. And he practices what he preaches. Maxwell was working with a pastor in Orlando, Florida, when he asked that question.

"Well, I know John Wooden," the pastor responded.

John Wooden, who passed away in 2010, is widely regarded as one of the greatest coaches who has ever lived. As the head basketball coach at UCLA, Wooden led his teams to ten NCAA Championships in twelve years. But Wooden was more than just a basketball coach. His teaching, wisdom, and inspirational messages made him revered by his former players, opponents, leadership experts, and the business world. Wooden was known as the "Wizard of Westwood," and his Pyramid of Success that he taught his student-athletes is widely acclaimed inside the business and coaching worlds.

So when Maxwell heard that this teacher knew Wooden, he got really excited.

"I'd like to know John Wooden!" Maxwell responded.

With an introduction from the pastor, Maxwell found himself preparing five pages of questions for the upcoming meeting at Wooden's favorite breakfast spot. That meeting led to another. Wooden eventually wrote the Foreword to one of Maxwell's books, and Wooden's quotes, wisdom, and stories appear in many of Maxwell's other books. John Maxwell considered John Wooden one of his greatest teachers and one of the most important relationships in his life. That relationship, though, would never have happened without asking that one simple question.

Maybe this inspires you to ask that question more.

Maybe this makes you cringe because you realize how many connections and relationships you have missed out on by not asking that question.

Or maybe this makes you realize that you aren't building deep enough relationships to feel comfortable asking this question. Because as powerful as this question can be, it will lose some of its luster if it's done without having a relationship first.

Pay To Get To The Front

"You have to invest if you want to progress." — ERIK HATZIKOSAS

Bill Konves has a growth mindset when it comes to collaboration as well as the value of our time. Konves, an avid sports fan, loves cheering on his Ohio State Buckeyes. But he has little patience for attending the games in a conventional way.

"I don't wait in concession lines at games," he told me. "Time is too valuable."

"So what do you do?" I asked curiously. "Do you not buy anything from the concession stands?"

"Not at all," he responded. "When I see a long line, I go right to the front. I start up a conversation with the person at the front of the line and ask what they are getting. I offer to buy them their food if they would order my food as well. Nobody turns me down."

With a unique idea and a gift for a stranger, Konves saves himself oodles of time, and some surprised sports fan gets their food for free. I thought back to how many special moments I missed at games because I was in line for food.

It's one of those simple life hacks that makes too much sense to have not known about. Think about how much goes into going to an event— getting ready, traveling in, parking, three or four hours at the game, and then driving home. Does it seem silly to spend all of that time and money only to be waiting in line when a pivotal moment in the game happens? As much as it costs to go to the event— in money and time— wouldn't it make sense to use a little more to bless someone else and get back to why you are there?

We can adopt that same mindset when it comes to investing in ourselves. Too often, we attempt to do it alone. Either we're too cheap or too controlling. What was interesting was that it was at a mastermind retreat that we both paid to be a part of when he told me this. At that multi-day event, I got to connect and build relationships with a variety of business owners who were also investing back into themselves.

I mentioned this in *Freelance to Freedom*, but at that event, I met Kyle Shultz, who owns Shultz Photo School. At that event, a collaboration between us was created and an online course came out of it. When that course launched, it brought in more than $52,000 in less than a week.

Initially, paying for that mastermind and that event gave me pause because it was a significant investment.

Later that week, I realized that I also had paid to get to the front. By making that investment, I bypassed endless wasted time and frustration trying to figure things out on my own, and it also opened doors to connect with other elevated and elevating entrepreneurs. By paying to get to the front, I put myself in the room that I had been waiting for years to be invited to. Not to mention how we are perceived by doing so. All of those people in that room take you more seriously because they know that you put your money where your mouth is.

Don't underestimate the value of paying to get to the front.

The Sneezers

"If everyone is moving forward together, then success takes care of itself."

— HENRY FORD

Kent Sanders is what I call a "sneezer." Charles Nicholls, founder of SeeWhy, came up with that term in 2010. But before you think he has an allergy or some virus, understand that being a sneezer is a valuable thing. A sneezer is someone who spreads the word about others. He is one of the rare ones who is often looking to spread information about those he trusts to benefit those around him.

It's not uncommon to find a thoughtful, unexpected gift from Kent in our mailbox for us or one of our kids. Yet Kent has had every opportunity to quit. You would have forgiven him if he wasn't in a giving mood. For more than a decade, he was a full-time college professor attempting to build his own business.

His entrepreneurial journey began in 2008 when he started blogging. But he had no clear focus and meandered inconsistently writing about a variety of topics. He consistently struggled financially while attempting a wide variety of business ventures to lift his family out of financial struggles.

One summer, he bought into a networking marketing business selling health products. After trying to drum up interest with no success, he gave up after a few weeks. The next summer he tried selling books on Amazon. As a college professor, he had shelves lined with books he wanted to get rid of. He listed, packed, and shipped the books to Amazon.

Kent made a few hundred dollars but the rest of the books weren't selling. Ironically, he ended up paying Amazon to destroy the rest of his inventory because it was cheaper than continuing to store it or have it shipped back to him.

Through these unsuccessful attempts at business, Kent always maintained a love for writing. That love was always with him, although he wasn't able to figure out how to make money from that either. Approaching Christmas a few years back, funds were typically tight. He had one client in his latest business of writing show notes for podcasters. A few weeks before gifts were to go under the tree, his only client told him that they would be pausing their services for a few weeks. Just like that, the money that kept them afloat was gone.

One frigid day, he checked his bank account to see that there was only seventeen cents in it with two weeks left until he would get paid from his job again. In a moment of pure desperation, Kent began looking for anything he could sell on Facebook Marketplace or Craigslist. Sitting there on the floor of his home office with a massive knot in his stomach from the stress, he vowed he would never, ever put himself and his family in this situation again.

It was around this time that Kent connected with Nick Pavlidis, a ghostwriter who also runs Ghostwriter School, which trains writers to learn that craft and build a business from it. The problem was that he didn't have the money to join and he lacked the confidence that he could make anything happen business wise.

Despite Kent's fear and his one figure bank account, he approached his father for a loan. Kent felt humiliated but his career path had become so painful that he had to make a push to do something that he really wanted to do. I got to watch this firsthand because it was around this time that he joined us in the *Total Life Freedom Mastermind Community* as a founding member.

Kent finally found his fit as a ghostwriter. His love for writing since childhood manifested into a blossoming career. If not for the failures and setbacks that he endured for years, it would be easy to say that he got lucky going from $15,000 per book project to now commanding $75,000 per ghostwriting deal. But Kent doesn't get these jobs simply because of his writing.

"Success isn't necessarily about being the most talented or gifted," Sanders told me. "It's about who has the best relationships."

But why does he have great relationships? We hear that often, but what does it mean?

Sanders is an amazing example of how being a connector and a collaborator lifts success to higher levels. Sanders is not only quick to respond but he's also quick to refer potential clients to us, to other writers and to those within his powerful network. Sanders has a natural interest in lifting up those around him. That's why I call people like Sanders "Sneezers"—people who spread the word about what you do. Without you asking, they will mention your business to others. They will introduce you to those who are a good fit for what you do. They send out unexpected, thoughtful gifts. They will be your raving fans, actively spreading the word about the value you and your business provide.

Sneezers should be treasured. They are the ones who deserve extra time and attention. You might have a lot of clients and connections, but few will be sneezers. They are either too busy, not connected enough, or don't yet understand the value of that role. But they are the ones who are wired to spread the word. It's imperative to identify, support, and value the sneezers in your tribe. Your network and your business will be stronger for it.

Become a Media Channel

"Here's what's exciting about sharing ideas with others. If you share a new idea with ten people, they get to hear it once and you get to hear it ten times."

— JIM ROHN

Do you love the idea of selling? Does the thought of promoting your work, your content, and your successes excite you? Do you feel little to no trepidation in sharing your gifts to the world on social media, to your email list, and in other ways?

Did you answer no to these questions? Would you be surprised to hear that I answered no as well? Because of my lack of love for selling and self-promotion, I have wondered out loud how I have made it in this world of entrepreneurship for so long. I do just about everything wrong when it comes to the "best practices." Unless I have changed my ways from the time I wrote this to the time you read this, I am classically bad in traditional sales, promotion, marketing, and every type of business jargon taught to make your business profitable.

Yet, each business we created— within multiple industries— has been deemed a success by all of our metrics. Not just financially, but quality of life for our family, our health, and our time freedom. One of the catalysts in this is the idea of becoming a media channel. Unlike the days of long ago— like 2007— we now have the control over becoming a media channel. It used to be that we hoped that a news station would do a story about us. Now, we are the news.

The beauty of this micro-niched world is that we each can create our own customized media channel and can do this with any and all of the media that resonate with us. It can be one or multiple outlets-podcasting, email marketing, social media, and many more which have the power to shape our very own media channel.

Do we understand the freedom that comes with this? Do we understand that we can use that channel— no matter how small— to report on, editorialize and share the influence of the world we are a part of? One of the greatest powers in creating your own media channel does not come from self-promotion. It comes from the vast opportunities to speak on the influences that have impacted your life and those of your network.

If this sounds confusing, think of it this way. A news station rarely discusses themselves. Sure, they effectively throw in commercials and the occasional internal promotions, but by and large, their content is derived from within their community. Most individuals whiff on this mightily, missing great opportunities in the process.

When you create a media channel, you create content that others are excited to share. You create goodwill by using your platform to lift those who have influenced you. You get to promote *them*, which seems much easier to do for those who don't enjoy promoting themselves. It allows you to build an audience that gives you the vessel to nonchalantly mention the things you do without feeling like a salesy, over-promoting hack.

And by making your media channel stronger, you build and lift up your network. You create a natural platform that allows you to promote your products and services in a way that feels organic, natural, and helpful to others.

It's the ultimate form of collaboration— and you don't even need permission to collaborate. By sharing the work of others and highlighting their stories, you build trust and goodwill while bringing attention to those inside your network. You can also do the same for those outside your network you admire. And there is no better way to get someone outside your network into your network than by generously sharing their message with your audience.

Business Is Personal

"All business is personal. Make your friends before you need them."
— ROBERT JOHNSON

There is an infamous scene from *The Godfather* where Michael Corleone creates a plan to rub out the rival mob boss and a corrupt police chief. Sonny Corleone, his older brother, laughs him off.

"You are taking this very personal. This is business, and this man is taking it very, very personal," Sonny jokes.

Michael gives his take— that this officer had it coming because he was tied up in drugs, corruption, and dishonesty.

"It's not personal, Sonny," Michael Corleone declares coldly. "It's strictly business."

From that moment on, the soul of Michael Corleone is corrupt. Before that moment, he was the one son who wanted nothing to do with the family business. His father, Don Corleone, the godfather, didn't want Michael to join the family business either. He had too much potential.

Michael left home to attend Dartmouth College but dropped out to join the United States Marine Corps after the attack on Pearl Harbor. Because of his heroic efforts in the war, he became a lieutenant and is awarded the Navy Cross and the Silver Star. After an assassination attempt on his father, the youngest Corleone reluctantly entered the world of the mob.

Through this trilogy, which has been lauded by actual mafia members for how true to life the movies are, Michael Corleone goes from being an American hero to one of the most notorious villains in film history. Although he calmly states in that iconic scene that,

"It's not personal. It's strictly business," that clearly isn't true. It's all personal. He makes the mistake of taking it *personally*. And it leads him to killing all of his enemies, including his brother. Still, his charisma leads him to convince his entire family otherwise.

That line— "It's not personal. It's strictly business"— has been recycled in the business world for the past fifty years. It justifies the impersonal side of business. The movie was made from the book of the same title, but a monumental scene from the book was omitted from the film, possibly changing business history.

In that scene, Michael Corleone has a different take.

"Don't let anyone kid you. It's all personal. Every bit of business. They call it business. But it's personal as hell," Michael Corleone says sharply.

The "It's not personal" line, which has been revered, has become a safe haven for treating rivals poorly. It allows us to believe that short-term benefits, which are one-sided, are normal business practices. It allows us to delude ourselves into thinking the work that we do— that we devote our time, our creativity, our ideas, our passions — isn't personal. But it is personal. It's all personal. And I've learned that getting involved with people who believe it's all business will never lead to long-term, collaborative efforts that become a win-win for the parties involved.

Michael Corleone was all business. Although rife with power, his grip tightened as he became greedier and more isolated. After ascending to control the mafia through ruthless business tactics, Corleone lost everything he craves and everyone close to him.

Business is personal. How we treat our clients, how we deal with the competition, how we collaborate with the connectors— It's *all* personal. Don't use the excuse that it's just business. That's an excuse you use when you know your ambition will hurt or upset someone else. It allows you to escape a charged-up environment you don't want to deal with. That answer is to your short-term benefit and yours alone. Like Michael Corleone, it may lead to near-sighted highs, but it will rarely, if ever, lead to long-term success. Referrals, respect, and relationships that have long-term benefits should always outweigh your short-term gains.

The Foundation to New Collaboration

"Each of you should use whatever gift you have received to serve others, as faithful stewards of God's grace in its various forms."

— PETER 4:10

Let me tell the story of how the design for the cover of this book, and the interior design, came to happen.

Our family moved to Bradenton, Florida in September of 2021. We had been feeling the pull to find a good church, since we were never able to find one that was right for us in Pennsylvania. After going to several churches to get a feel for what was here, Elizabeth heard about the Oasis Church. The first day that we arrived, there were food trucks everywhere. During the service, we learned that day was literally their ten year anniversary.

In celebration, pastor Steve Coad brought in food trucks with burritos, açaí bowls, barbeque and ice cream, and it was all free.

"Best church ever," I said.

The next week, as the month-long celebration continued, it was free pizza. That "best church" label stayed. This continued all month. Our loyalty would be tested when the first Sunday without free food would arrive. You'll be happy to know that our souls stayed intact when we didn't leave after the free food left.

During that first food bonanza, Anthony Casto introduced himself to our family. Outgoing and talkative, he helped us feel welcomed right away. He went out of his way to introduce us to his family and be curious about us, our children and what brought us to Bradenton.

After feeling alone at so many of the churches we went to, it was so nice to have someone go out of their way to make us feel welcome.

A group of families at the church often meet on Thursday nights and we decided to join. It was during those evenings that we learned more about each other, our past history, our struggles, and what we do for work. I mentioned that I was working on this book and Casto explained his current work at a school as well as his time as a designer. He had worked for years designing magazine layouts, covers, interior design, and much more. The schedule- and the demanding bosses- eventually led him away from that career. I had someone lined up to work on this book cover so I didn't think more about it.

He showed me his work, which I was impressed with, and he inquired about how my book was coming along. Remember, *those who ask the questions control the conversation.* One evening, we were discussing concepts of design as well as my book. Anthony's passion was evident as he threw out ideas. He wasn't looking for anything but to help and connect. He didn't know that the work that was being designed for this cover wasn't getting me excited. There just wasn't a "fit." I was frustrated by the process and unsure what to do next. The clock was ticking.

It was then that I opened the door to a possible collaboration. I made sure there were no guarantees and we met after church to discuss concepts. After one meeting, he got to work. I hadn't even hired him yet. He didn't care- he was excited to begin creating. That evening, I received a mock up version of a potential book cover. I made suggestions and he made tweaks. I heard back from him right away. It still didn't click but I was enjoying the process of working with him. Anthony was energetic, attentive, and extremely coachable.

Even if the designs weren't clicking yet, there was little doubt that we would get there if this continued in the same manner. Throughout the collaboration, I realized, through conversations with Anthony, that I wanted something much simpler than I was originally imagining. *The Wealth of Connection* is a fairly simple concept. I wanted the cover design to reflect that. That can be hard for a designer because they want to showcase what can be done design-wise. Anthony helped me pare it down to fit the feel. Often, simplicity is the best method. Before we knew it, the cover was designed. It went so quickly that we didn't even discuss the price until it was complete.

The next step was the interior formatting. I asked if he did that as well, and he said he didn't format books. The following Thursday night, he brought his laptop to our home. He asked again about what I needed and he realized that not only could he do it but he had extensive experience formatting. We were just using different industry terms. Working together in the dining room, after most of the guests had left, we worked in tandem to get the design elements down for the interior of the book. Again, it took one day to decide and again, it moved so fast that price wasn't discussed. We made sure that it was set before he left to make sure he was properly compensated.

I told him how serendipitous it was and how our connection modeled the path of *The Wealth of Connection*. He did so many of the right things. He initiated the conversation. He was curious and asked meaningful questions. To a fault, his generous goals were placed over his own selfish goals. After getting to know him, I trusted his character. With the foundation of character and curiosity, the connection was easy and natural. Without any pressure, that led to a seamless collaboration. I compared this to all of the research we did trying to find the right person. The portfolios and web searches. The delays in communication and lack of bonding on styles. Finding the right person can be the biggest challenge.

Yet, this worked so easily. I believe it's because the foundation of *The Wealth of Connection* brought this together personally. Now I get the opportunity to use my platform to put him over.

The Value of Collaboration

When people think of words to describe entrepreneurs, the word *collaborators* isn't one of the first that comes to mind. Instead, entrepreneurs are thought of as loners who work on their own, in their office, creating their own masterpiece. The reality is that the great ones— the ones who don't hightail it back to the corporate world in frustration— are adept at sharing concepts, thoughts, and ideas. They value feedback from others who give honest opinions.

They are the ones that go out of their way to lift up those in their network and go to different worlds to connect with those outside their network. And they know the true value of having a powerful network. They have confidence that what they create is valuable, yet know that collaboration with others creates better ideas, stronger strategies, and unique visions or products.

These entrepreneurs know where their genius zone is. They also know where it isn't. So, working with others who fit will make things better for all parties, allowing each to shine in their area of expertise. They believe in helping helpful people and know that gratefulness not only feels good, it opens doors. They've learned how to apologize, how to follow up and how to build trust before asking for a favor.

The greatest entrepreneurial minds are not driven by competition and world domination but by the drive and the satisfaction of what collaborative relationships really can do.

Part 5

CREATION

Value Growth More Than Engagement

I want you to envision where we are at this point. Your **Character** is established. When you enter conversations, you aren't word vomiting about yourself, your business, or your beliefs. You don't have an agenda or an angle about how others can help you. You actually listen when people talk instead of thinking about what you will say next. When you leave most conversations, the odds are people don't know much about you. Why? Because most people engage selfishly. They are so deprived of attention—or are self-involved—that they use that time to talk about themselves. Yet, near the end, they backtrack and say, "But I don't know anything about you!"

At this point, your goals are generous. You look to connect others even when they look to do nothing for you. When you are faced with tough conversations, you are generous with your honesty. You may lose friends, but the friends you have will value the truth. You are putting your generous goals above your selfish goals, maybe for the first time ever. You have figured out, after being fooled and confused, that charisma is not character. You realize that most people are so wrapped up in themselves that they don't care about what you are working on, yet you still give standing ovations to others. *And you feel better doing all of this.*

You have figured out that **Curiosity** may have killed the cat, but it's revitalized you. You ask better questions. You are more interesting to others because you are curious about them. You have learned that being shy is indeed being selfish. You understand that everyone knows something you don't, and that anyone can help anyone else with something. You now ask yourself if you are trying to be interesting to others or interested in others. And you realize that it's best to think like a beginner.

It has also hit you that you are in the **Connection** business. And even though we are more connected online than ever before, we are lonelier than ever. The average adult male has the equivalent of less than one true friend. You understand that endless connections and one great idea is better than endless ideas and few connections. You read the room, know what to say when you do talk, and are adept at listening. You now name names, keep in touch, and respond quicker. And you realize you can do it all in The Hour of Giving. You now connect the unconnected, you go where you are celebrated, and you understand that at this point, all you might receive for it is psychic compensation. Yet you still do it.

You now know that **Collaboration** doesn't happen and isn't sustained without great Character, Curiosity, and Connection. You now look to collaborate instead of compete. You know that building a powerful network is of huge value. You know it's going to take a year, and you work on success by association rather than guilt by association. You put people over, receive feedback better, and understand the value of giving a real apology. You not only connect with other worlds, but you also bring those worlds together. And you are becoming a media channel to let those worlds know about the people in your network and their remarkable achievements.

Now Let's Talk about You

"Success is the progressive realization of a worthy goal or ideal."
— EARL NIGHTINGALE

For 80% of this book, we've focused on what everyone else needs but very little about what you want. If you are still here, that means you have what it takes. The selfish ones are gone already. We haven't discussed how *you* will benefit from all of this, but I suspect you see the good that comes to your life by shifting from selfish goals to generous goals, becoming more curious, developing meaningful connections, and creating collaborations from those connections.

But deep down you might be wondering, "What about *my* stuff? What about the income I want to create? The business I'm trying to build? The book I'm looking to publish? The podcast, blog, or platform I'm looking to grow? What about me?"

I saved this for last on purpose. Almost everyone is focused on themselves. That's why they are frustrated, disconnected, and underperforming. Accomplishing selfish goals works for a while. The author of *Black Sheep* and keynote speaker Brant Christopher Menswar explained his experience well during a lunch together.

"Chasing my personal goals got me to a certain level of success in the corporate world, but it wasn't until I got there that I realized there was a limit to what I could accomplish on my own. It wasn't until I focused on my relationships, collaborations within them, and serving others that I learned my success could become unlimited."

If you buy into what we've discussed so far, your Character, Curiosity, Connections, and Collaborations are in place—or at least are on their way. It takes a year, remember?

The rest of the way, we're going to focus on you.

Build It And They Will Come?

"Build it and they will come is not a strategy. It is a prayer."

— STEVE BLANK

I struggled with where to put the Creation part of *The Wealth of Connection* because it easily could have gone earlier in the book. We are always creating, and oftentimes it's the first thing we look to do. How many times do you hear about someone who has a business idea, or someone who has developed a product, or a person that on a whim starts a podcast? Or our ten-year-old Dylan creates a new generator, portable cooler, or desk fan based around cardboard on a near-daily basis. Creation comes at all times and in many forms. It's not a linear thing.

Yet, I put Creation at the end for a reason. In order to make an impact, you need to have Character, Curiosity, Connection, and

Collaboration in place first. I spent years trying to create some type of a platform. I obsessed over titles, fonts, and logos. I tried to build the websites (I should never again try to build a website) and I tried to follow all the things I saw influencers in my industry doing and what the coaches were saying. I toyed around with a few podcast ideas that went nowhere. I created a blog that fizzled out after a few months. I had dozens of book ideas, course plans, and membership ideas. It seemed as though I spent more time brainstorming and dreaming than anything else. The ideas seemed solid after running them by some friends for validation. Even looking back, some of those same ideas—even down to the titles—were done by others and became successful platforms.

Yet idea after idea faded away to obscurity. I spent years listening to podcasts for motivation, dreaming that I could do what these people were doing. We had a business that was successful, so I wasn't desperate to make it happen—not unlike someone reading this with a job that pays the bills. The work is "good enough," yet you know you'd like to do something more impactful with your life.

But where in the world do you start?

There is the famous line from *Field of Dreams* that says, "Build it and they will come." It's an amazing movie line, but it's terrible business advice. The world is littered with frustrated souls because they built it and nobody came. You only hear the success stories from the people who made it through the fire. The unfortunate truth is that history is written by the winners, and those who didn't win fade away.

We hear inspirational stories about those who made it. What we don't hear are the stories of those who failed because they gave up and settled on being realistic. They are the ones who say it can't be done and are more than willing to tell you why you can't do it either. What they don't do is explore *why* it didn't work. Excuse-makers aren't curious. That lack of curiosity is the first sign of why. Often, it's a combination of all of the things we've previously discussed. In one form, or in all, there is a deficit somewhere in their character, curiosity, connection, and their collaboration.

Show me someone who is strong in those four areas, and I will show you someone who will be successful when they put something out in the world. How can they not? If they have good character, they lead with integrity. If they are curious, they are interested in others and can create products and services that fill their needs and wants. If they are great at connection, they develop solid relationships and a powerful network that jumps in line to support them. If they enjoy collaboration, they will work with people who bring the skills, knowledge, resources, and connections that they don't possess. Now tell me, is that person primed for success when their creation hits the open market?

All that's left is creating what others are waiting for.

But before we move on, let's take a look at those who only paid attention to their own wants and needs. They spent their time so focused on what they wanted to create that they spent little to no time being generous to—or curious about—others. Their selfish ambitions kept them from building meaningful connections that led to amazing collaborations. And because so little of that was in place, when they created something, they were met with baffling disappointment. The amount of people who have come to me because they created a course that nobody bought, wrote a book nobody read, or had an invention nobody supported was one of the initial reasons I decided to finally write this book.

Fail at Something Cool

"What is the point of being alive if you don't at least try to do something remarkable?" — JOHN GREEN

Are you afraid of failure? Does the idea of failing strike up fears of embarrassment? If so, you are not alone. Most people have a fear of failure. We were actually *trained* to fear failure. What do you think school was all about? It wasn't about trying something that you love, being encouraged to make tons of mistakes so you can learn and grow, and continuing to improve your craft through problem-solving. It was about getting an A on a test to get you into college, so that you can get more A's so that you land a good job and your guidance counselor can say they placed you into a good school. To do that, failure is discouraged. If you fail a test, you go to the back of the line. I knew I didn't enjoy school, but I didn't really understand why until I was out in the real world.

In the world of entrepreneurship, failure is embraced. Failure is necessary to understand what success even is. Learning and growing happens when you fail, not when you cautiously look for the right answers. So students become so afraid to fail that they only look to get things right, which stunts innovation and creativity. There is the joke that in the real world: the A students work for the B students, the C students run the businesses, and the D students dedicate the buildings. If you doubt the truth in that, go ask the A students out in the working world and judge their reactions.

I was most certainly a D student. I'm not on pace to dedicate any buildings yet, but I am running the businesses. And I certainly did fail in school. A lot. I got so used to failure that it barely fazed me any longer. I came to expect it, so much so that I became numb to it. I didn't mind the failure, but I also didn't realize how to utilize it. I got a little *too* used to failure and allowed myself to try and fail at things I didn't even care about. Failure became so common that I associated myself with it, affecting my confidence and self-esteem. What I learned was that so many failures meant I no longer had any expectations. Consistent failure will do that to a person.

When I looked back, I noticed that not only was I failing on tests, I was failing in life. So I had no expectations when I started my first freelance business. The dream career seemed so unattainable that I told myself I was probably going to fail, and why not? Up until that point, I'd failed at everything I tried. Most of those things I didn't enjoy doing anyway.

But I told myself, "If I am going to fail this time, I'm at least going to fail at something cool."

And that statement gave me a blank slate to go and do what I wanted, which is the reason it worked. Because I was going to do what I wanted, I gave it everything I had. And, of course, there was no expectation attached to it. It wasn't until a few years ago that I realized how often that came up in my life. With my history, there was no reason to think that I could write a successful book. No teacher ever encouraged me to be a writer, let alone have the audacity to get a publisher and endorsements from best-selling authors and businesspeople. Who was I to think I could do that?

When I went to write a book, it sounded cool. There weren't expectations. It's probably going to fail. It was the same for creating everything else we created. If I had put pressure on myself to make it succeed, I don't know that it would have turned out this well. But knowing that it's probably going to fail, people are going to see it fail, and the sun will still come up the next day? That made it much easier to try. The more failures you have, the less they sting. I try not to think about the failures I've had because I prefer to spend my time on things I thought were going to fail but actually worked.

So go and try something. Don't be like everyone who does something for the money or because their mom said they should do it. They fail in the worst way because it's something they *didn't* want. But when you continually choose what you want to do, people will wonder how you get to do so many cool things. And it will be because you chose to fail—and fail at something cool. And when you learn, grow, connect and get better, you actually won't fail as much. Then you will see that your work life is amazing precisely because you get to do all those cool things.

So go fail at something cool.

It's All Bonus

"There are only two ways to live life. One is as though nothing is a miracle. The other is though everything is a miracle." — ALBERT EINSTEIN

Does it all seem overwhelming? Does the idea of taking control of your life and creating the work you love seem frightening because if you fail, there is so much more to lose? Are you one of those overthinkers? One of those who worries about making the wrong decision and screwing up everything going forward? What if I start this and it's a massive failure? What if nobody buys it and I get totally embarrassed? What if I spend all of this time, energy, and money only to fail and then realize that I'll need to start over again?

As a teenager, I was convinced I wouldn't live to see twenty. I said it to myself and I said it out loud without much thought to some of my friends. Even though I did it to myself, the decisions I made, the friends I chose, and the rapidity in which trouble entered my life convinced me I would die young. It led to a sad end to my teenage years. No job was taken seriously. Neither were most relationships.

One day during my senior year in high school, I was drinking whiskey in the woods across from our school with a few friends. I was drunk before classes began, so we skipped the early part of the day. We wandered down to the train tracks to avoid any passing teachers or students who might rat us out. As the sun rose higher over the tracks, we noticed the rumbling of the oncoming Long Island Rail Road train rounding the bend and heading for the Roslyn station. I didn't notice that everyone hopped off the tracks and gathered along the rocks a safe distance away.

But not me.

I'm not sure if it was the whiskey, my sadness, or a combination of the two, but I didn't move. I sat on the tracks staring at the train coming at me. My friends were calling for me to run, but I didn't hear them. Everything seemed muted and distorted. I don't remember hearing anything, including the train. I unemotionally stared at the front of the train as it chugged closer. Quite honestly, the only thing that crossed my mind was that if I wasn't here any longer, my mother would probably be the only person who missed me.

Between my friends yelling and the repeated blaring of the train's horns, I mentally snapped back. The train was getting close, but for some reason I still didn't hop off the track. Finally, after realizing that my thoughts about not living until twenty had nothing to do with me ending my life intentionally, I stood up and jumped away moments before the train would have gotten me.

A few years later, I visited a friend in the hospital. She was getting her appendix removed. Her family, whom I hadn't met before, was there. We engaged in small talk, and at some point it came out that it was my birthday. The conversation switched to me as they all wished me a happy birthday. It suddenly dawned on me that it wasn't just my birthday, it was my *twentieth* birthday. I got lost in my mind for a moment as I realized what happened.

"I never thought I would see twenty," I told her mom. She seemed confused. "I never thought I'd live this long."

I drove home not long after. As I exited the Meadowbrook Parkway and merged left onto the Northern State Parkway, the darkness of the night seemed almost bright. I wasn't supposed to be here. I never thought I'd be alive to see this. Only one thought crossed my mind. A thought that quite literally changed my life.

It's all bonus.

I wasn't supposed to get this time. All throughout my teens, I felt angst for being a loser. A failure. A waste. But that was okay; it would all end soon somehow. Yet, when I made that turn onto the highway, I knew in my heart that not only was that part of my life over, but everything I had beyond this was all bonus. All extra. No expectations. And more importantly, no reason to stop myself from attempting anything I wanted to accomplish.

I am proof that your life can change in an instant. Although I didn't snap out of all my awful habits immediately, they were being emptied out quickly and being replaced by positive energy, ambition, and a brighter hope for the future.

Instead of stress, feel freedom. Instead of worrying, seize the opportunity. Instead of regret, see potential. Remember that the odds of even being born are effectively zero. You had a one in 400 trillion chance of even making it into life alive. *You aren't even supposed to be here!*

It's all bonus. Live like it.

Start with a Following

"A leader is best when people barely know he exists, when his work is done, his aim fulfilled, they will say: we did it ourselves." — LAO TZO

Do you believe that it's all bonus? If you do, it's time to get moving. What's there to lose? It's all bonus, remember?

When I finally understood *The Wealth of Connection* was when I focused on the first levels of Character, Curiosity, Connection, and Collaboration instead of what I was creating. I looked back at the successes in my life and recognized that each one took place when all four of those levels were in place before Creation took shape. The times where things were confusing, frustrating, and lacking momentum were when I tried to rush the content and creation without building out those four foundational pieces. I tried to push something through because it would benefit me most, and I wasn't curious what others thought or needed. I had no connections and obviously little opportunity for collaboration. Each time that happened, I'd think back to my story about shooting the pope and once again see how similar my position was to that.

Whether it was getting access to high-profile events in photography, writing books, creating an online course, publishing the *Total Life Freedom Podcast,* and starting the *Total Life Freedom*

Mastermind and Community, it seemed like whatever we touched found relatively quick success without any marketing. *Freelance to Freedom* launched with more than one hundred Amazon reviews right out of the gate. That happened without a following, an email list, any marketing, paid (or unpaid) ads, and a grand total of five social media posts regarding the book prior to launch. The sports course earned more than $52,000 in a week simply due to the right collaboration. The podcast hit 10,000 downloads in the first two months and now has more than 700,000 downloads. And like the book, it received more than a hundred reviews in short time. Again, there was little to no advertising or promotion. The Mastermind and Community replaced our previous photography income with a fraction of the work needed—also in a short time frame.

They were all built on the foundation of *The Wealth of Connection:* Character, Curiosity, Connection, and Collaboration.

So what was the difference? Why was there such a drastic change from the years of toiling in frustration attempting to build a platform to seemingly everything working with (embarrassingly) less effort? I finally understood that I needed to change my character from one focused on selfish goals to one focused on generous goals. Now, I would have *said* that I was generous then, but looking back, I can see that I simply paid lip service to it. I did what I needed to do to get what I needed to get.

Going from selfish goals to generous goals was the cornerstone to turning everything around. Next, I dove deeper into my curiosity. Fortunately, that was usually there with me. But curiosity from generosity helped me learn so much more about people, which made *me* more interesting to *them*. Who knew? That naturally led to deeper connections and relationships, which is the most important part of this. Screw this up and you will constantly face pain and failure. Get this right and your connections will lead to meaningful collaborations.

So guess what happens when you focus on those four foundational tools before you focus on selling your stuff? You get to start with a following. When you start with a following, people trust you because you have proven yourself to be someone who cares for others. And people who already love what you do—that is, when you finally put your content and creations out into the world—are a tribe of people in your corner. Entrepreneurship isn't easy. But when you start with a following, you have laid the foundation for success and significance.

The Passionate Few

"Fans, true fans, are hard to find. Just a few can change everything. What they demand, though, is generosity and bravery." — SETH GODIN

If you have excuses as to why you can't build a business that earns you the income you need, provides the time and location freedom you desire, and provides the opportunity to impact like-minded people in a positive and encouraging way, you need to leave those at the door. You can't take excuses any further on this journey. Because everyone has a combination of passions and expertise that can lead to that life for them.

Gone are the days when we needed someone to choose us. When I graduated high school, the only opportunity for income I saw was to go to a business that was hiring, fill out and submit a paper application and hope they would choose me. Of course, it would all be on their terms. The hourly or salary rate, the work hours, the location, the working conditions—everything up to them.

It couldn't be more different today. We no longer need one person or one company to pick us so we can make a living. Those looking for traditional employment are in that camp, but it's the polar opposite for the entrepreneurs of the world. So often those venturing into the entrepreneurial space get discouraged because they either don't have a big enough following or they feel they need to build something that will be universally loved.

Somehow you have found this book. I am grateful to you for

taking your valuable time to read it. Even though I have your attention right now, I must tell you that I do not have a huge following. Of the 7,800,000,000 people in this world, 99.999999% have no idea who I am or what I do for a living. Another very small portion of those people know what I do but don't need it. A smaller portion knows what I do, might need it, but doesn't care or don't trust me yet. An even smaller portion knows what I do and know they need it but won't pay attention or pay money for it. And an absolutely minuscule portion that knows what I do goes forward and works with me.

Yet I get to sit here and write this book while somehow living a life that has total financial freedom, our family can live and work from anywhere, and I get to do only the specific work I love with the exact type of people I enjoy working with. Now, how do you build that life for yourself when it seems like hardly anyone knows you or cares about what you do?

You do it by focusing intensely on the passionate few who actually do care. They are the ones that need you to solve their specific problems. They are the ones you obsess over helping. They are the ones who will give you detailed questions to answer. They are the ones you focus on. They are the ones you look to connect within your network. They are the ones you lift up, promote, and make successful. They are the ones that get overserved and become raving fans that spread the word about you and invite their friends.

You don't need a huge following. You don't need the followers, the big stages, and the hype. You just need a passionate few.

How to Play to an Empty Room

"I wish I would have started when nobody was listening." — BEN KILLOY

In 2013, I was asked by an organization in Cleveland to give a keynote speech about the creative side of business. They had a large number of people in their group, and the number of potential attendees was exciting. I booked it, worked on the speech, and had everything ready before the trip to Cleveland.

As I walked into the room, I realized, as a new speaker, this would be the biggest crowd I had ever spoken to. I arrived two hours before the speech to meet everybody and get my nerves together. Within minutes, I chatted with the man running the event. The conversation went by so fast that before I knew it, we were an hour out until I was to go onstage. Fifteen minutes later, I noticed that only one other person was in the building. Concern crept in as I realized that I was to go on stage in forty-five minutes and there were two people there and two hundred empty seats to fill.

Thirty minutes before showtime, there were a grand total of three people in the building. All three were looking to talk to me, but I couldn't pay attention because I was feeling pretty insecure right then. So I thought positively. Maybe they're arriving in busloads and they are about to arrive. With twenty minutes to go, there were four people in the room, and nobody seemed to be in a hurry. It was then that the organizer informed me that someone forgot to send out the promotional emails to let everyone know that I would be speaking that night. He apologized and promptly wished me luck. Only two more people showed up.

I was about to speak to one hundred ninety-four empty seats and six filled ones. A total of twelve eyeballs would be looking at me during the ninety-minute presentation that I spent weeks preparing.

I don't know if it's embarrassment I felt. Maybe it was fear. But I remember being on the stage with a lump in the pit in my stomach. I just wanted to leave. I considered turning around, going through that back door, and driving straight home. I'd just pretend that nightmare never happened. It was at that point that the guy who ran the organization came up onstage and introduced me. He was one of the six people, and the audio guy was another. So there were four people who actually showed up to see me.

As my first slide was displayed on the big screen behind me, I began the presentation. The first minute was awful. It was awkward. It was embarrassing. One of the six people was on their phone. It was a nightmarish scene moving in slow motion.

I paused and took a deeper breath while leading with a story that fortunately got everyone laughing. With a little momentum built, I realized that I had their attention. Ten minutes in, I no longer felt stress. There was no worry at all. It didn't matter if there were six people or two hundred. In fact, it was actually fun talking to six people because I got to make eye contact with every one of them. The small crowd allowed me to do what I wanted without worrying about impressing anybody because there was hardly anyone to impress.

In the end, I was thrilled that there were only six people. It proved to be a great testing ground. What was funny was that I got to talk to each person after the speech, which you don't get to do with a big crowd, and every one of them gave me their insights and feedback, and two of them emphasized that the others were going to be so disappointed that they missed it. What started out with great anticipation moved to something with a tremendous amount of sadness and disappointment. Then it ended on a high note because it didn't matter how few people were in the room. It was actually a good thing to start small.

That experience was crucial in the growth of my podcast, online course, membership, and everything else. I might not have started the podcast without that experience because I might have mistakenly thought that I needed a certain amount of people to listen or I needed to be at a certain level to start.

That free speech for six people turned into more free speeches, which improved my content and confidence. Those free speeches turned into paid speeches. Those paid speeches turned into higher-paying speeches, which turned into even higher-paying speeches.

Whatever your creation, you may start by playing to (nearly) empty rooms. How you play to that room will be what determines your success. And what is the best way to play to an empty room?

Do the best you can for the smallest amount of people and obsess over creating and serving your true fans no matter how few they are.

The True Fans

"Pleasing a true fan is pleasurable. It rewards the artist to remain true, to focus on the unique aspects of their work, the qualities the True Fans appreciate." —

KEVIN KELLY

All potential customers are not created equal.

Kevin Kelly pointed this out brilliantly in his 2008 article *1000 True Fans*. Kelly's article, which has been updated consistently since it was first published, is a manifesto for creative entrepreneurs both new and experienced. He contends that artists and creatives don't need a million followers. You just need a thousand true fans. He describes a true fan as someone who will buy just about anything you create. If you are a musician, they will drive to your concert and buy your music. Whatever your art is, they are buying.

So if you produce enough each year for them to buy $100 worth of material, all you need are 1,000 true fans to make a good living. If you are thinking long term, then you need to create one new fan per day. In three years, you will reach a thousand true fans. That's not counting word of mouth, referrals, and anything else that helps you grow. It's also not counting fans that are not so super (meaning the ones who buy occasionally).

At the same time, a thousand true fans who pay $100 is just one part of it. What if you have a hundred true fans who pay $1,000 per year? What if you have a $500 product or service with 2,000 true fans? What if you have a subscription service based around your micro niche that is $100 a month? If you create 100 true fans who pay you $100 a month, you have just figured out how to earn a $10,000-a-month recurring income stream.

Kelly's point is to focus on your true fans because true fans will also bring in and attract casual fans. True fans have value in many ways. Not only are they the first to buy, but they also become your marketing team. Think about the things you are a true fan of. Do you want to keep it all to yourself, or are you excited to spread the word? Do you want to be alone in your excitement, or do you want to be part of it with your friends?

The idea of gaining a thousand (or a hundred) true fans has never been more doable. Given how connected we are online, and how even the most obscure item can be placed next to the most popular item online, even the most obscure niche product has a way to be found. As Kelly states, if one in a million people shows interest in what you have, that is potentially 7,000 potential true fans. And it's likely your odds will be much better than that.

Kelly concludes that instead of chasing stardom, create a thousand true fans as a solid path toward success. By doing this, you aren't concerned with having a bestseller, or a viral video, or any other desperate or ego-driven path to success. Instead, you simply connect and serve your true fans. You won't have to sell out and do marketing and promotions that are the "flavor of the month" to attain instant success. Focus on your true fans, and give yourself a much higher likelihood of succeeding.

Why Does Anyone Need That?

"Choose the niche that you enjoy, where you can excel and stand a chance of becoming an acknowledged leader." — RICHARD KOCH

Have you ever come across a product and asked yourself, "Why would anyone need that?" Of course you have. We all have. And that used to be true—before the internet changed everything. But the days of the small business owner marketing to the masses are over. It's too expensive, it's too inefficient, and it's way too impersonal.

Now it comes down to you. You have an idea, but your friends and family ask why anyone needs that. I had a close family member try to understand the world of online communities and masterminds that I run. After I explained the business model, this person innocently responded, "People pay you for that?"

They didn't get it. And they shouldn't. It's not for them. And it's not about what your mom thinks someone needs. It's about crafting a specific, niched idea to a very small group of people who get it. And that is all you need. It's not surprising that your brother-in-law doesn't understand why entrepreneurs looking for an online community based around building a membership site would pay to be a part of Shane Sams' Flipped Lifestyle online community. Your brother-in-law isn't one of them. He doesn't get it, and he doesn't need to.

"Why would anyone need that?" is really just a person saying that they don't need that, so in their narrow worldview, no one else will either. It's bad enough when we blow off other people's ideas by saying, "Why would anybody need that?" but it's much worse when we say it about ourselves and our ideas. Because we are selling ourselves short.

After coaching so many on this, it's pretty universal that we undervalue our experience, passion, and knowledge. Why do teachers accept low pay, long hours, and frustrating bureaucracy while catering to the masses as opposed to choosing a specific niche tutoring what they are the best at? The one subject that lights them up and makes people eager and willing to pay them?

How about the photographer who "shoots everything" in order to pay the bills? Why not choose an exclusive group of clients that can afford what you do and are willing to compensate you for bringing something so personal to the project that they wouldn't think of hiring someone else?

Or that giving soul who so badly wants to help their struggling friend find financial freedom but is met with blank stares, excuses, and pushback. So they continue banging their head against the proverbial wall, frustrated that they can't break through to this person, in time questioning their own ability to impact others and turn it into a business. They can see that their friend needs help, *but their friend doesn't think they do.*

So we tell ourselves that nobody needs it, but we must realize that some do and will recognize that they do. And that's all we need. We don't need many to make it work—not if they're the right people. The truth is, people *do* need it, even if it's not the people who already know you.

A Business By Surprise

"Chance is always powerful. Let your hook always be cast: in the pool where you least expect it, there will be fish." — OVID

"I wasn't even looking for a business," Dan Miller explained.

It's funny how some of the best products, businesses, and books are started by accident. Dan's book, *48 Days to the Work You Love*, wasn't created from his overwhelming desire for riches, to be a well known author, or to have a huge platform. In fact, he didn't want the work he was doing to make any money.

Dan was raised by a Mennonite pastor in a very legalistic, non-attention seeking way. There was no pride and no promotion in his upbringing. It was a household where they received a pair of blue jeans, and nothing else, as a Christmas gift. As a teenager, Dan had different beliefs and broke away to pursue his own life. That included marrying Joanne, his wife of 54 years, which was frowned upon by his family because she didn't share the same faith. A serial entrepreneur, Dan never had a problem making money. Throughout their marriage, he had his hands in a wide variety of businesses. So chasing the dream career was the furthest thing from his mind.

Instead, he chased personal development. That came in the form of teaching career transition to members of his church. That passion eventually led to him spending up to thirty hours per week coaching these members with no income derived, and none sought after.

Even though he was a successful entrepreneur, the idea of charging for his ministry was never a thought because of the way he was raised.

But because he was spending so much time doing it, Joanne told him that if he was going to spend so much time doing this, it should have something to do with his income.

Dan struggled with this. Because of his upbringing, he felt that he should never do something like that. It would be viewed as manipulative to turn your ministry into a money generator.

During that time, Dan would fly to England for three weeks at a time while continually working on his Doctoral program from The University of Oxford.

"While I was in England," Dan told me, "Joanne would field all of the calls from people wanting to see me for coaching. Eventually, she began saying that I could see them, but it was $345, and I had a spot on Tuesday at 4pm. I came back home, and she handed me a schedule. 'You have paying clients', she said!"

"You've got to be kidding me," Dan responded. "This is my ministry. I wasn't looking for business. But the business showed up in what I was already doing based on my heart's desire and my desire to serve. It became a business by surprise."

"Yet once I started charging, they were like, 'You aren't just a nice guy at church," Dan explained. "You are a professional! And that has never stopped. It was like a dam broke when I made it a business rather than just being a nice guy."

What started as a little program teaching Sunday school class had become a real business. Someone in that class told Dan that his son-in-law needed to hear what he was saying. This man asked what he could give to his son-in-law to learn more. But Dan didn't have anything to give to him. Because of those requests, Dan put together a rough compilation of his Sunday school notes inside of a three ring binder. To add value, Dan added two cassette tapes filled with additional content.

In 2002, as he was putting this together, he saw that Mark Victor Hansen, the author of *Chicken Soup for The Soul*, was giving a conference in California about how to sell books.

"My approach has always been to learn from the masters," Dan said. "The conference was $695, and I told my buddy Dave Ramsey about this. 'You've got this little book, *Financial Peace*, that you are selling out of the trunk of your car. We should go!"

Dan, Joanne, Dave, and Sharon Ramsey went to the conference together. In the next thirty months, Dan sold more than two million dollars worth of that three ring binder with the cassettes inside of it. For the perfectionists reading this, all of those sales were just from the rough material.

"From there, publishers started calling," Dan explained. "You see, everything I have done has been counterintuitive to how people normally approach this. Now, people have a book and they want an advance and guarantees. Forget that! Do something that has value, get it out there, and if the market says that it does have value, you can't stop the progression of that."

That binder turned book- *48 Days to the Work You Love*- has sold more that 1.2 million copies to date.

"I never searched for a publisher," Dan concluded. "They showed up from the success that we were already having."

Be a Conduit

"Skills garner acclaim but character gains trust. Opportunity and loyalty go to those who have both." — KEVIN MILLER

It really doesn't matter which level you're at in your career—there is a good chance perfectionism is holding you back. And when I say perfectionism, I don't mean what you have to do needs to be perfect. What I really mean is that you are scared to put yourself out there for fear of judgment and criticism.

Are you insecure about how you show up on video? I can relate. Do you hate the sound of your voice? Join the club. Do you tell yourself, "I'm not a writer?" I did. Are you afraid your message is not clear enough? Do you feel like you are not the "authority" in your field? Therefore, who are *you* to do this?

Does any of this sound familiar?

Zig Ziglar was the premier motivational speaker of his time, and even years after his death, he developed an almost cult-like following, with his work still teaching many. And as successful as Ziglar was, he struggled with those same questions. Before he walked on stage, he questioned his voice. He fretted over how he appeared. He wondered if he was the right choice to deliver his message.

But he figured out a way to get over all of it so he could go out there and impact the audience. He realized that when he worried about being perfect or feared criticism, he was only thinking about *himself*. How he would be perceived. Essentially, it wasn't about being perfect. It was about his ego. But was it really about him? The breakthrough for Ziglar was realizing that it wasn't about him. It was about the message getting to the audience.

It was then that he knew that he needed to be the conduit. A conduit is a channel something can pass through. If he was a conduit who didn't have to be perfect, it didn't matter if his message wasn't perfect. It made no difference if he didn't look ideal. Conduits aren't known for their style. Conduits are the vessels through which information flows.

And that's what Ziglar became: a conduit for his message. By being the conduit, he could no longer hide behind the veil of perfection. He couldn't use the excuse that he didn't like his voice, that he wasn't happy with how he looked, or that he wasn't the be-all, end-all expert in his field.

By being the conduit, none of that stuff mattered. As long as he was the vessel that information could flow through, his job was done. Each of us needs to remember that it's not about getting the credit. It's not about how we look or sound. It's not about us. It's about us being the conduit to get the message out to the right people in the right way. That's all that matters.

A Million Micro Niches

"Nobody goes there anymore—it's too crowded." — YOGI BERRA

You are in an amazing spot. What you have at your fingertips is the potential to create whatever career—and life—that you want. It doesn't matter what age, gender, race, or color you are, or even what disability you are dealing with. For the first time in history, you can create whatever life and income you want, and you don't need anyone else's permission to do it. The number of online businesses that earn solid income without us even knowing who the owners are or what they look like should make you feel like you have no limits. These businesses are often run from a phone in their pocket that has more computer power than Ronald Reagan had at his disposal as President of the United States of America.

We, the people, hold the cards. Even though we still have major corporations that control much of the business world, that has been fracturing at a rapid pace.

Micro niches are quickly multiplying and are eating away at the foundations of these big corporations. And it is the same with the media. The major news organizations that we believe have all the influence are being beaten in the ratings by individual podcasters and YouTubers. It's a real-time example of how the micro niche is taking over. Ratings for these major networks are dropping even though people are consuming more content than ever. They are just following the micro brands now.

What's different is that the big players can only do so much, and they often can't go deep (with content) or specific (with product). What does that leave? A big, gaping hole for each of us to carve out a tiny niche that we can own. Humans have a much wider variety of interests than big corporations, brands, or media can serve. Anything you can think of, there is a niche created or being created to serve that specific audience. Everyone's an expert in something, no matter how obscure. And if you aren't an expert yet, I'm sure you have a deep interest in something. That's where the idea of a million micro niches comes in.

If you are still trying to figure out what you can create, get curious. What area isn't being served? Maybe it's health. Now, that's a very broad topic. There are tons of big businesses and micro niches accounted for. How can you niche down? Is it in the form of fitness? A certain skill you possess that would be unique to the industry? With everyone going online, can you create something more local? What can you do differently that will stand out? How can your interests add a unique flavor? What is needed but underserved?

By creating something specific to your skills, interests, and expertise, and in an area that others need, you attract people that only want what you have created. They will not want anything that is broad or general. This is how you stand out.

And this is why it's so exciting to work in a world of millions of micro niches.

Avoid the Curse of Knowledge

"The curse of knowledge: When we are given knowledge, it is impossible to imagine what it's like to lack that knowledge." — CHIP HEATH

Lee LeFever, the author of the book *The Art of Explanation,* talks about the "curse of knowledge." The idea behind it is that we often get so wrapped up in ourselves that we forget to step back and see things from our potential customer's point of view.

"The more you know about something," LeFever explains, "the harder it is to imagine what it's like not to know."

And that can be dangerous. Before you even have a single customer, the curse of knowledge can derail you if you allow it. We often don't value what we know, since we assume that if we know it, others know it as well. So we downplay our expertise by thinking people won't be interested. Or we don't even see it as a viable skill because it is second nature to us.

But what we think is ordinary, others think is extraordinary.

Some areas where you have the curse of knowledge could be turned into a viable opportunity. I'm convinced more and more that we all have one. Where we often get stuck is that we don't see ourselves as an expert, or we think that some other expert should lead. True, you might not be an expert compared to the person two steps ahead of you, but you certainly are the expert compared to the people that are two steps—or more—behind you. You have already been where they want to go.

Unfortunately, our default setting is to compare ourselves to the "top dogs." When I started as a business coach, I doubted my abilities. Even though I had done everything my first client was hoping to do, I had tremendous insecurities about being good enough to coach. I went as far as to say that to my client.

"I'm not sure I'm qualified to coach you," I admitted. "I am certainly no Tony Robbins."

"Hey," he said back, giving his own coach a pep talk. "I can't afford Tony Robbins!"

And there you have it. That one little line set me straight. I was further along than he needed me to be, and he couldn't afford to hire me if I were at a higher level. It made me realize that there is always a place for what we can do, whether we are beginners, intermediaries, or experts. If you are a beginner, there are many ways to get compensated. Simply gaining knowledge by teaching will make you better, get you testimonials, and build referrals. You might even make a little money. As you rise up, so do your rates. But you don't need to be the expert to lead the person who is just starting out. Don't underestimate the knowledge and expertise you possess so that you don't fall prey to the curse of knowledge.

We are becoming a culture of micro tribes, and we all can claim a stake in our own niched, exclusive world. That means that we need to let go of comparison and build our own world. We need to have enough courage to take what we have and build that tribe. Carve out the exact niche you will be serving, and become steadfast in making sure it is for them and them only.

The Long Game

"Our patience will achieve more than our force." — EDMOND BURKE

I *suck* at marketing. I'm talking epic levels of suckiness. I don't promote what we offer well, I'm not consistent with marketing, I don't enjoy the idea of branding. Deep down, I just want to create my work and connect with cool people. That's really it. Personally, I like myself best- and I enjoy my work best- when I don't have many financial goals. In the simplest form, I just want to enjoy what I do.

Yet, I have friends who have strong integrity with their work, focus deeply on relationships, and market so much better than I do.

John Ruhlin is one of them. I connected with John in 2016, when his book *Giftology* was released. I resonated with the book and the message so greatly that I asked if he would endorse *Freelance to Freedom*, which he graciously did. We stayed in touch, I ordered copies of his book for friends, and I joined his email list to stay informed.

In 2019, I received an email from John saying that he was throwing out the first pitch at a Cleveland Indians game and he had an extra ticket in his suite that night, and he was giving it to someone on his email list. I responded immediately that I would love to be the one. John responded minutes later, telling me that he has always known me as a giver, and the ticket was mine.

After Ruhlin threw out the first pitch, I enjoyed the evening surrounded by not only John, but his business partner, tons of his friends and associates, and even his adorable daughter. When I saw how many people were there, I figured that I would get a few scant minutes with him at best. This wasn't my first "suite" get-together, consisting of schmoozing, small talk, and little real connection.

To my surprise, after saying hello, we talked for nearly forty-five minutes. I started feeling guilty because there were so many important people in his life that were there, and not only did I get his undivided attention but it was deep and meaningful. He was so open and personable that I had to ask a specific question.

"How do you stay so focused on growing the brand of *Giftology*, when you devote so much time to great conversations *and* you have so many ideas of other things you can do?" I asked. "How do you stay so focused on this book and not get distracted by writing another?"

"If it was up to me, I *would* be writing the next book- or books!" he said. "But he (pointing to his business partner) keeps me in line. As many ideas as I have, *Giftology* is the anchor to our business. Hal Elrod (the author of *The Miracle Morning*) taught me to not just have a book launch, but to have a five-year book launch."

An anchor is the main- and most important thing- that you offer.

I had not heard of a five-year launch before. In fact, I was guilty of doing the opposite. When my first book launched, I went all-in for a few months. I allowed the next idea- and ideas- to get me excited and get myself bored with my own book. Subsequently, I stopped talking about it. I stopped marketing it. The conversation was so interesting that I asked him to discuss this for *The Wealth of Connection.*

"Most people do the flavor of the month thing and then move on to the next project. My book is evergreen. It's my anchor. It's crazy because authors spend two, five, even ten years writing a book," John continued. "But it's all about the long game. Either in relationships or in your work. If you write a book, this is your bible. Why would you not treat it that way? Hal (Elrod) told me that it took five years for *The Miracle Morning* to gain momentum."

The Miracle Morning has now sold millions of copies. Imagine if we gave our anchor, as Ruhlin describes, a five-year plan? How much more focused would we be? How much more of an authority would we be in our field of expertise? How much of a different impression would we make then we do by endlessly switching to the next flavor of the month?

Because of his five year plan, Ruhlin can focus on making an impression that most can't- or don't. Ruhlin set out to do something special for his friends, associates, and people he admired from afar. He did something that so many people thought was crazy. For the first fifty copies, he spent $250 apiece to make a one-of-a-kind product that would not only make these people feel special, but also would make a lasting impression. All fifty copies were handmade out of leather, monogrammed to them and their spouse, placed inside of a monogrammed leather bag, then placed inside of a linen box.

As amazing as that was, what was even better was that he didn't ask for anything- not even for them to promote the book. He did it to say thank you. But it was so unique and impressive, one of the most influential people in book publishing not only invited John onto his podcast, but bought copies for his entire team as well.

A five-year launch never lets you get bored. John is always looking to improve *Giftology* because it isn't a one-and-done product. He has versions 2.0, 3.0 and beyond. Instead of new and shiny, he simply focuses on making his anchor better.

"Most people's long game is in days," John concluded. "My long game is decades."

The Content Waterfall

"A strong person and a waterfall always carve their own path."

— UNKNOWN

Consistency and creativity don't always go together. But when you find people who master it, do your best to make them a part of your board of directors. There are few people that I know that balance their worlds of consistency and creativity better than John Stange. John appears so unflappable that I finally asked him if he ever gets mad. He laughed and responded with a self depreciating affirmation that he absolutely can lose his cool.

"What does it take?" I asked.

"It's simple," John said. "Lie to me."

Because of his stellar reputation is his community- and the online communities that he is involved in- I would imagine that doesn't happen often. And because he doesn't allow drama into his life easily, that frees him up to do what he does so well: create amazing content with an impressive level of consistency. John is a part of our mastermind, and I'm regularly impressed by his ability to take the anchor that John Ruhlin spoke of, and turn it into multiple forms of content that don't require a crazy amount of time but give him a reach of content that hits multiple platforms including podcasts, blogs, videos, and more.

John calls this his Content Waterfall.

John is the lead pastor for the Core Creek Community Church in Langhorne, Pennsylvania, and creates and writes a sermon that he gives every Sunday morning. For most pastors, it ends there. But not for Stange. Either he is one of the most organized and consistent entrepreneurs I know or it's that he is one of those annoyingly rare people that only needs a few hours of sleep each night because he doesn't get tired. Or maybe it's a combination of both.

Either way, it's a winning combination. Here is what he does. After writing the sermon for the week, he starts his waterfall. The content is already created, worked out, and organized. Now it's time for it to flow down like water speeding down Niagara Falls. When that water initially descends over those falls, it has a ridiculous amount of momentum, power, and force. He treats his sermon the same as that water.

Where most creators let that water stagnate into a puddle or pond (if you are looking at yourself, be comforted in knowing I am looking at myself as well), John creates his own waterfall. The text from the sermon is immediately turned into a full-length blog post on his website, giving his website tremendous search engine optimization for new people to find him. He takes the same entry and posts it to various publications, including Medium.com. John turns that content into an email newsletter. From there, he takes the audio from that same sermon and turns it into an episode for his *Dwell On These Things* podcast or a part of his *Platform Launchers* membership. The content from that same sermon is turned into multiple social media posts, giving traction and visibility all over the internet. That same content is also turned into the future books that he is writing.

Does the visual of the waterfall make more sense now? He creates one piece of content and pushes that content downstream, where it is used in so many different ways, for people who enjoy the content but consume it in different ways.

If you have a podcast, there will always be people who would prefer to read a newsletter. If you have a newsletter, there are people that will always prefer to watch a video. If you create videos, there are always people that would prefer to read a book. If you publish books, there are always people that would rather read a blog.

For so many creatives, creating content for all of those platforms sounds overwhelming and exhausting. But not if you have an anchor and create a waterfall from it. Because for John Stange, once that sermon is created, the content for these other platforms is created. It's just a matter of separating and distributing them to other channels.

Now that he has taught us about the content waterfall, he now needs to teach us how to thrive on just a few hours of sleep. I need my eight hours, so the content waterfall seems much more doable.

Don't Break the Chain

"We first make our habits. Then our habits make us."

—JOHN DRYDEN

Consistency could have been its own section for *The Wealth of Connection*. You can have great character. Yet as Will Rogers notes, it takes a lifetime to build a reputation, and that reputation can be lost in a minute. Your curiosity can get you out of a jam when desperate, but consistent curiosity unlocks a youthful, magical view of the world that can't happen in fits and starts. Anyone can gain value from connection and collaboration when they are in the mood to be social, but the person who makes connection a habit builds a powerful network that opens a world of possibilities. And content has been known to be caught like lightning in a bottle. Consistent, dedicated creation can have a massive impact, as in this next story.

There is a decent chance that earning a great living with your content is of high value to you if you are reading this. There is also the chance that you've made a decent number of mistakes in your journey so far. It has been said that we learn from our mistakes, but we benefit by learning from other's mistakes as well. It's also wise to learn from other's successes. So, do you want to learn from a creator who earned $51 million in 2020?

Jerry Seinfeld is one of the most successful comedians of our time. What is the one word, when his success is studied, that was most responsible for his astounding career accomplishments?

Consistency.

It's easy to get "into the mood" of creating when it feels right. It's just as easy to make an excuse when you aren't feeling it. But it's consistency that separates the pretenders from the ascenders. And Seinfeld mastered his domain in consistency better than he did in one of his most famous episodes. So what was his secret?

Shortly after the TV show *Seinfeld* became a hit, comedian Brad Issac was working the same club as Seinfeld one evening. Issac, a beginner, asked Seinfeld if he had any tips for him.

Issac shared the advice that the now-famous comedian shared with him in a *Lifehacker* interview.

He said the way to make better jokes was to create better jokes, and the way to create better jokes was to write every day.

He told me to get a big wall calendar that has a whole year on one page and hang it on a prominent wall. The next step was to get a big red magic marker. He said for each day that I do my task of writing, I get to put a big red X over that day.

"After a few days, you'll have a chain. Just keep at it and the chain will grow longer every day. You'll like seeing that chain, especially when you get a few weeks under your belt. Your only job next is to not break the chain."

"Don't break the chain," he said again for emphasis.

This new habit will be kryptonite for your perfectionism. Or procrastination, since they are essentially the same. Seinfeld didn't tell Issac to write the perfect joke daily. He said just make sure he writes a joke every day. One bad joke daily leads to one good joke every once in a while. Over time, with consistency and confidence, it leads to better and better jokes.

If you don't stop, you might end up with a body of work that is unparalleled in your industry, connections that one can only dream of, and a bank account that would have been unimaginable during your days of procrastination, perfectionism, and bad habits.

Be a Magnet

"Passion acts like a magnet that attracts us to its source. The more you discover and express your passion for life, the more irresistible you will become to others." - BARBARA D. ANGELIS

A great creator should be like a magnet. Magnets use their invisible magnetic field, which is a basic form of nature, much like gravity and electricity, that pulls similar objects to itself. A magnet does more than attract, though. It also repels. Repelling those away who are not a great fit is an important part of creating your following.

For people who don't mind confrontation, this is an easier path than it is for people-pleasers. People-pleasers tend to want everyone to like them. For the record, I am not a people-pleaser. Confrontation does not make me uncomfortable, and I will argue that the need for confrontation is necessary. By not confronting the people who need to be repelled, you will get dragged down with negativity and drama. I can still love them, but I'll love them from way over here while they are way over there. Too often, we don't want to do the hard work of pushing away the wrong people before it's too late.

How do you repel? The most preventative way is to do it from the very start of your messaging. In business, some leaders miss this from the start by saying that what you do is for "everyone." As someone looking for a unique community to join, the fact that it is for everyone turns me off right away. So you want to be careful not to repel the right people. Saying anything is for everyone is a surefire way to repel the right people and quickly attract the wrong people.

But by being specific, you quickly bring in the exact type of people you want. And how do you repel? Being crystal clear in your language is an essential checkpoint for keeping the wrong people out. When it comes to *Total Life Freedom Mastermind*, we are clear that this is a group of generous, engaged, action-taking entrepreneurs who are working together to build a life of time, money, and location freedom. Why did we word it this way? Well, it wasn't this clear in the beginning. But through time and experience, we realized that this needed to be for entrepreneurs and aspiring entrepreneurs. People looking for this type of freedom weren't looking for full-time jobs. By doing so, it eliminated much of the frustration that came from the employees who didn't have time to work on their business. We're either going for this or we aren't.

Another part of the language that we make clear is that this is a generous group. So when I interview someone hoping for a spot that has opened, I am forward when I ask what they are going to bring to the community. Some people are taken aback by the question.

"What will I add?" they ask. "I am applying because I need help from you."

"I get that," I let them know, "but if everyone is just looking for what they can get and they aren't looking to make the people around them better, then it's not much of a community."

That always gets the point across. It is interesting how quickly the applicant rethinks their approach and then reassesses how they love to encourage others, participate in one-on-one conversations, and have a particular skill or mindset that can benefit the group. Once that is established and clear, we are closer to accepting the right members.

Being a magnet allows you to pull in and attract those who resonate with your message, repel those who aren't a good fit, and build authenticity and boldness in your messaging and your content.

Don't Pretend to Be What You Aren't

"Don't fake it till you make it. Be real, be transparent, be authentic and be yourself." — DARREN HARDY

Being different doesn't mean being more successful. It means being who you are—which often creates that success.

You might have noticed that it says non-bestselling author on the cover of this book. That may seem like an odd way to market a book. Why did I decide to put that there? Because it's true. The book world is a space where everyone wants to be a bestselling author. Apparently that leads to credibility, more sales, bigger stages, and ultimately more money. And with thousands of books being published daily, the fight to be noticed is more fierce than ever.

And in the fog of needing attention, authors are looking for any advantage they can get to gain credibility. And undoubtedly being a best-selling author will be the thing that gains that validity. It started years ago with the *New York Times Bestsellers* list. Algorithms were figured out to find out how many book sales were needed to make the esteemed list. There are authors who have spent up to $300,000 to get their books on that list and still didn't make it.

They pulled out all the stops. There are ways to get just a few people to buy in bulk but ship them to thousands of individual addresses to make it look like a thousand people bought the book. Can you see where this was going? As the internet expanded, the information became more known. It got worse once e-books became part of the game. Again, certain people figured out how to game the system. Once you know how it works, it becomes possible to buy your way onto the list.

If you think that's bad, that was just the beginning. Once it was no longer about actual book sales, other places realized it would be wise to get into the game of awarding bestsellers. It wasn't long before many other news organizations had their own bestsellers list that could then be compromised. You probably aren't surprised that an entire industry geared toward authors wanting their book to be a bestseller rose like a phoenix. They created categories in the most obscure areas—basket-weaving bestseller anyone?—to assure that every book can become a bestseller if you follow their plan, which is built upon everyone purchasing through their business.

Brent Underwood was tired of this entire thing. He decided that he was going to prove how silly it was by becoming a bestselling author. Underwood became an Amazon bestseller by investing just two dollars and uploading a photo of his foot. It took less than five minutes. He explained that he really wasn't in the mood for writing a book. So, he took a picture of his foot and titled the fake book *Putting My Foot Down*. Underwood then submitted the masterpiece to Amazon and a few hours later, *Putting My Foot Down* was up on Amazon. He placed it in the category of the widely sought-after Transpersonal Psychology. He then texted one of his friends asking if he would buy the book. In the first three hours, it sold three copies: one to his friend and two to him. Later that evening, Brent Underwood was a number-one Amazon bestseller and did a quick screenshot before it all went away.

Even before I started writing *The Wealth of Connection*, I knew that non-bestselling author was going on the cover. Why? Because I am not a bestselling author, and I refuse to play a vanity game all for a title I didn't earn.

Just because something is being done doesn't mean you should do it. We blindly chase the bestselling author role or whatever meaningless title your industry chases without wondering if anyone really cares. Nobody really cares. They care about how your work can help them. They care about how the message resonates with them. They are hoping to be inspired, educated, or entertained by your work.

But they don't care about awards. That is about your ego and your need for validation, not the impact you are creating.

Find Humor In It All

"To make mistakes is human; to stumble is commonplace; to be able to laugh at yourself is maturity." — WILLIAM ARTHUR WARD

On April 24th, 1974, the city of Tampa was awarded a coveted franchise from the National Football League. After the excitement faded, they were tasked with fielding a professional football team from scratch. Unlike today's generous rules for new franchises, the expansion draft had the Tampa Bay Buccaneers choosing players from the bottom of the barrel. Their options were to choose aging veterans, castaways from other NFL teams, and drafting unproven rookies. There was a lack of medical attention for these players, so the uncertainty on their injuries or medical history contributed to their issues.

As was the case, the Buccaneers became the first team in NFL history to go an entire season without winning or tying a game. And it was even worse than that. They didn't score a single point until the third game of the season, and they didn't score a touchdown until the fourth. They didn't score a point in nearly 40% of their games that fateful season. At the end of the season, they were ranked last in the league in touchdowns, rushing touchdowns, and points scored.

John McKay was their sarcastic, wise-cracking head coach, and after winning three NCAA National Championships at USC, he wasn't used to the bumbling, inept play he inherited in the NFL.

One of McKay's most famous lines occurred during that 1976 season. After yet another brutal loss, a reporter asked McKay, "What do you think of your team's execution, coach?"

"I'm in favor of it," McKay responded.

At the end of the season, McKay made a declaration.

"We'll be back. Maybe not this century, but we'll be back."

McKay sold himself and the Buccaneers short on that joke. Three years later, almost to the day of that statement, Tampa Stadium was rocking with a sold-out crowd as McKay and the Buccaneers ran through the tunnel and onto the sun-drenched field to battle the Los Angeles Rams for the NFC Championship for the chance to play in Super Bowl XIV.

The point I'm attempting to make—if it wasn't lost on an obscure football story—is that when you start, you will not start with the best resources. You won't have the best talent around you. You won't have the experience to make the decisions to get yourself to your "championship," whatever it is. McKay had a long-term vision for the Buccaneers. Winning the championship in 1976 wasn't the goal.

He needed to develop a vision, a culture, and a standard that would be entrenched once they could recruit and draft better talent. He knew it was going to take time. He also knew that you needed to have a sense of humor when going through the beginning. During a press conference, he chided reporters by telling them that they didn't know the difference between a football and a bunch of bananas.

When he showed up for the next press conference, there was a case of bananas by the door.

"You don't know the difference between a football and a Mercedes-Benz," McKay responded.

We all experience rejection. We're all going to experience the crickets that come with an unsuccessful effort. If you put yourself out there, you will meet the critics. You will take on projects that don't go the way you hope, and some people will pounce on your perceived failures. It's important to laugh at ourselves and have fun with it. McKay's ability to do that won over his critics, bought him time and grace, and afforded him the ability to stay in the job longer to gain the experience to coach a championship game when just a few years earlier, they went a full season without winning a single game.

Pressure and Time

"The first step is to establish that something is possible. Then probability will occur." — ELON MUSK

The Shawshank Redemption might be my favorite movie of all time. I can count on one hand the movies that would get me to stop in my tracks, drop everything, and plop zombie-like onto the couch if it's on the screen. In the movie, Andy Dufresne is wrongfully imprisoned for the murder of his wife and her lover and ordered to serve two consecutive life sentences.

Two years into his sentence at Shawshank Prison, while etching on the prison wall in boredom, a small piece of the wall falls loose. Dufresne, who loves geology, quickly realizes this might be the solution to his unjust imprisonment. Over the next twenty years, he appears to be the model prisoner. Because of his banking and accounting prowess, he is enlisted by the warden to keep the books and shield money in various banks throughout Maine. Within the prison, he is well-known and liked by just about everyone.

But he keeps a secret that isn't found out until one morning when he isn't in his cell for roll call. The warden panics when he realizes his prized prisoner— the one with information about his illegal financial activities—has vanished from his cell overnight.

Only, it isn't a magical flash that got Dufresne out of prison. In the dark of night for twenty years, he chipped away at the wall, removing tiny pieces of it. Each day, during his walk outside, he emptied his pockets of those pieces.

When his friend Red recalls how Dufresne did the impossible, he cites his love for geology. Geology is simply a matter of pressure and time. That's all it takes. Pressure and time. It's no different with what you are creating.

The world is filled with get-rich-quick schemes and people who are ready to fall for them. It's also filled with entrepreneurs who want instant success, consumers who want the magic pill, and prisoners who want to get out as quickly as possible. And very few of those ever end well. Yet, when we use the concept of pressure and time, fulfillment and success are unavoidable.

Seth Godin has one of the most popular business blogs in the world. It didn't happen because of a gimmick, a trend, or a hack. It happened because he published a blog post every day for more than 10,000 days. Godin said that not one of those blog posts ever went viral. What he did was use the same method Andy Dufresne did in carving his way out of prison.

The myth of overnight success destroys momentum. We have all daydreamed about what we would do if we won the lottery. But nearly one-third of lottery winners file for bankruptcy. In fact, lottery winners are more likely to file for bankruptcy within three to five years of winning than the average American.

Between constant money requests from friends and family and selfish encounters with those around them, good friendships and immense fortunes are destroyed due to someone else's sense of entitlement when the rightful winner receives their fortune. Being flooded with cash after years of having little, as well as not having an understanding of how to handle it, leads to catastrophic financial mistakes and painful life lessons. Overnight success leaves one unprepared for the barrage of attention that comes with it.

Creating A Mic Drop Moment

"The best advertising is done by satisfied customers." — PHILIP KOTLER

When I was twelve, my childhood friend Howie Tessler invited me to his house to watch a recording of a professional wrestling match that took place a few nights earlier. I knew nothing about professional wrestling until that night. On the screen was the start of a steel cage match between Jimmy "Superfly" Snuka and the "Magnificent" Don Muraco.

They fought a bloody battle inside of the cage at Madison Square Garden and I couldn't turn away as Snuka climbed to the top of the cage, leaping twenty feet into the air with his arms stretched out, crushing Muraco into the mat. It's a memory still etched into my brain and one of the most iconic in professional wrestling history.

The Garden was the home for monthly World Wrestling Federation events (now World Wrestling Entertainment) and eight months later, Howie and I had gotten ringside tickets. The main event that evening was a no holds barred match between the patriotic Sgt. Slaughter and the villain The Iron Sheik, playing off of the ongoing conflict between the United States and Iran. The build up for the main event was electrifying and our seats were right against the gate where the wrestlers entered the arena.

I could barely contain my excitement as the main event was about to be announced. But before the Sargent and the Sheik battled to a bloody finale, ring announcer Howard Finkel stepped to the center of the ring. The microphone descended from the ceiling, and he announced the date of next month's event. The noise of the crowd went silent as Finkel began informing us of the matches that would take place the following month. Each match seemed better than the last, and Finkel dramatically worked towards the championship matches. People all around me had pens and paper, writing down all of the information. They had obviously done this before.

"In the main event for the evening," Finkel exclaimed, "Greg 'The Hammer' Valentine will battle Hulk Hogan…"

We couldn't hear anything else after that as the roar of the crowd raucously approved the upcoming battle for the heavyweight championship. He then announced that tickets would go on sale at the box office immediately after the event ended. They wisely gave the crowd a few minutes to make a decision and gather up their money, and Howie and I did.

"If we get separated after the match," Howie said, "meet me at the box office!"

As any patriotic story should end, Sgt. Slaughter took out The Iron Sheik. On his way back to the locker room, we were fortunate to snag the small American flag from Sgt. Slaughter's hand, complete with his blood on it. I was stunned when it eventually dried and we saw that it was real blood.

As soon as the match ended, Howie and I ran through the hallways of the arena to get in line for the opening of the box office. We battled hundreds and hundreds of people all vying to snag tickets. It was an amazing scene to see the hallways *after* an event packed with people as excited as they were during the event.

It was one of the most effective methods of word of mouth marketing that I have ever seen. I had never been so excited to give my money away. We were lucky to get tickets, along with 18,000 others. The event sold out right away. There was no internet marketing back then. There was no advertising. All they did was give everything they had for their most faithful fans, time the offer perfectly and give their true fans the first opportunity to buy tickets. By the time fans in the crowd and those watching on cable television had a chance to buy, there were no more tickets left for the not-so-faithful fans. I only remember saying one thing to Howie as we waited in line to get those coveted tickets.

"If we leave here with our money," I told Howie, "*then we lost.*"

If you create a product or service that gets your clients to say that line, you have created your very own mic drop moment.

The Magic of the Unique Blend

"Everyone wants to make a difference. But nobody wants to be different."
— ANDY ANDREWS

How excited would the average candy lover feel if you handed them a regular piece of milk chocolate? I think the level of excitement would be relatively low. What about if you gave them a glob of peanut butter? Not excited for that either, you say?

Yet, by some estimates, the Reese's Peanut Butter Cup is the top selling Halloween candy in the United States. Separately, peanut butter and chocolate are your run-of-the-mill staple products for your cupboard. But when these two are blended together, it creates a unique product that sells more than $500 million worth of product every year.

Blending two distinct, quality items is a formula for success.

My nephew, Michael Nania, experienced this firsthand. He's had a love for the New York Jets football team since he could remember. Michael studied every game with intense detail. My cousin, Vivian, and her husband, Mike, encouraged his passion, but they acknowledged that they were concerned that his love for the Jets would distract him from his studies. He excelled in math, and his parents didn't want to see him slip behind because of his passion for sports. They fretted over how to approach this.

But while they were worrying, Michael was writing. He developed an interest in his early teenage years and a penchant for scribing stories about his favorite team. But they weren't your typical rah-rah fluff stories. His stats-driven stories were outside the norm, and people began to notice. As a sophomore in high school, Michael took to posting his articles on blogs such as *Gang Green Nation*, where his work turned the heads of fans and other writers. At one point, one of the Jets beat reporters got caught using some of Michael's work without giving proper credit.

For Michael, school was never interesting. He knew what he loved, he was developing his expertise and passion, and he has the stubborn trait that runs in our family. So he graduated high school and tried a year of community college but never stopped writing and studying every Jets game. And when I say studying, it's the type of study that makes his history teacher ask why he couldn't study like this for her class. But why wouldn't he do this in school? Simple. He didn't care about what they were teaching. Those studies didn't go toward his passion or skillset. But combining the Jets and math? It's the Reese's Peanut Butter Cup of sports journalism. Robby Sabo had been following the work of Michael for a few years when they teamed up to create Jets X-Factor—a membership site to blend film study and analytics—to bring the Jets fandom an inside look that even the team itself can't provide.

The blending of skills in many aspects is what makes Mikey so unique. On a macro level, he combined his love for the Jets and math, but on a micro level, he went deeper. In the world of sports scouting, you have the stats people and the film people. Because of his love for the game, Michael blends both for a perspective that is unmatched.

Through his ability to blend, he created his own world where the possibilities are exciting and endless. A uniquely nuanced paid membership geared toward a rabid fan base in the nation's biggest city? Can you say potential? If the Jets were smart (let's not assume they are judging by their consistently inept results), they'd put him on staff to give them a viewpoint that is most certainly needed.

But before he reached the age of twenty-one, Michael showed that by focusing on his passion and his skill, he could create a product that stands alone and stands out. And being that these topics—the Jets and math—are extreme passions of his, the odds of success are so much greater. Not only is he one of the few built for this type of work, but his passion for it is so deep that he created a niche career that put him far ahead of the curve.

The Future List

"Even though the future seems far away, it is actually beginning right now."
— MATTIE STEPANEK

The problem for us creatives is not that we don't have a great idea to build upon. The problem is that we have *too many* great ideas. Anyone married to a creative entrepreneur can attest to the frustration of a spouse who has endless new ideas, the next always being the "one." Whether it is captured on scribbled notes throughout the house, written on receipts and envelopes, or revealed by the telltale sign of endless purchases of new domain names (people like this collect domains the way some of us collected baseball cards as kids).

Is it possible that having the ability to come up with great ideas can be a bad thing? It is if it's not controlled. It's not the collection of ideas that is troublesome, though. It's allowing the next sexy idea to derail us from actually making progress on one idea. Because we don't need a million things to work—we need one. One successful idea will solve most problems.

But how does having too many ideas hurt? It hurts because it creates too many distractions to make that one idea work. Every idea in the beginning is exciting. It is the quintessential honeymoon. It's not very different from a new romance. The rose-colored glasses are on. The dents and scratches are brushed aside by the newness. It's the same with a new business idea. It's new, it's fresh, and it has endless possibilities with little apparent downside. But as the development progresses, the bliss that comes with this idea becomes less shiny.

And that is where the danger comes in. Serial idea creators are like the person in a relationship with a wandering eye. As the flaws of the new partner become more clear they are drawn to the new thing. The daters of the world who engage in this carousel of new romantic endeavors attest to a constant source of adrenaline, excitement, and uncertainty but little stability or growth. It's not a way to develop a serious relationship—or build a successful business idea.

The solution is simple: choose. Commit to *something*. You will make more progress by sticking with one idea and growing it than keeping your hands and thoughts on multiple projects at the same time. But what do you do with all those other ideas?

I call it The Future List.

The Future List is my haven for ideas. It's my fire safe where I can store all the things I can do in the future. This list has simultaneously given me more peace of mind and excitement for what lies ahead than I ever anticipated. For starters, it gives me the relief that my ideas will not be forgotten. It also gives me assurance that I do not need to act on any of these ideas right away. They are stored for me when I need them. When I get excited for an item on The Future list, I simply pull up the document, write in any notes and thoughts I have, and leave it be.

With all these ideas stored, I have no shortage of future projects, which keeps me calm. I have more than enough ideas to work with going forward. The key is that I need to focus on what matters now. What is the thing I am going to do successfully now so that I have the time and resources later to build the next exciting thing on the list? It allows me to have optimal success with the knowledge that the future is brimming with possibilities.

One final thought. As you build your future list, your new ideas get better and more developed since you gave them time to mature. Each time that you go back to that document to add thoughts, the idea is strengthened. If and when you choose that idea to develop, you have a head start with content and ideas behind it. And just so you know, *Freelance to Freedom, The Wealth of Connection,* and the *Total Life Freedom Mastermind* were all future list ideas I wasn't ready to develop when the idea first came to me. It was only through years of adding ideas and content behind them that I was able to go after them with full momentum when the time was right.

The Turbo Button

"The time spent building a solid foundation will pay for itself ten-fold."

— DARREN VARNELL

I don't believe that technology always leads to improvement. My kids will never get to experience what it was like to walk down to the pizza place, grab a slice and a drink, and gather around the massive, stand-up video games with their friends for hours on end. It was our ritual during lunch, free periods, and after school. Armed with just enough quarters to last the day, we rotated in and out on who was playing next.

Technology has made it so easy that we rarely gather in person any longer. Even though we progress technologically, those memories of playing games together are magical. The two places we gathered during our high school years were the Pizza Pub and Nat's, the candy store next to the Pub. We would bounce back and forth, depending on the game and if we wanted pizza or candy. At the Pizza Pub, there was a baseball game we couldn't get away from. I'm not sure if it's because they were one of the first to use the names of real players and their stats, but we couldn't get enough of it.

Nat's—the name of the grumpy owner who yelled at us while throwing in some off-colored humor—had two games. When he brought in the driving game with different levels, cities to drive through, and special options to soup up the car, we were hooked.

I was frustrated because I kept getting beaten in that game. I couldn't figure out how to use all the options the car had, so I finished last most of the time. There was something called the turbo button which blasted out nitrous oxide and gave the car a major boost to either catch your opponent or pull further ahead. I hadn't figured out how to use it well. I seemed to always push the turbo button at the wrong time. My nemesis, Bobby Hubbard, always seemed to use the turbo button at the right time. While I floundered, using it too early in the race, Bobby held out.

I watched him while he played against our friends. He never panicked. He ran his race, not looking to win early. He got everything set up, developing momentum and confidence. He made sure he didn't burn out his tires or overheat the engine. He wasn't ahead often during the race, either. But while everyone else frantically tried to get ahead, Bobby ran his race discreetly. And then I saw it—it finally hit me what he was doing.

When his opponent was starting to fade—their turbo button already used, their engine close to overheating, and their brakes and tires low—Bobby was perfectly set up. All of his facilities were in great shape. And he still had his turbo left since we were only given one per race.

As the race got into the most crucial stage, it was time for Bobby to hit the turbo button. With his opponent on the ropes and his own car gaining momentum, he slapped that button, blasted ahead, and left all of us in the dust for the easy victory.

Most frustrated content creating business owners do the same as what my friends and I did. Most hit the turbo button too soon. Whether it's trying to grow an email list, creating a viral video, building a funnel, getting popular on social media, developing their message, connecting with influencers, or any other way to speed ahead.

Tom Schwab hit the turbo button too soon. Before you feel too bad for him, his business, *Interview Valet*, is absolutely crushing it. In many ways, Tom isn't the best example for this because his character is strong. He is so curious that each time I see him at a conference, we have an impromptu chat that is so engaging because of his questions. He is very well connected and has boundless collaborations. In the beginning, he was offered a spot on *Entrepreneurs on Fire* with John Lee Dumas, one of the biggest podcasts in the entrepreneurial world.

He hit the turbo button too soon.

"My message wasn't ready yet," Schwab admitted. "My business structure wasn't set. I reached this massive audience, but I got on to the show too soon."

A giant mistake many entrepreneurs make is trying to "get on" too soon. They attempt to hit the turbo button too quickly. We need time to create the message and hone it. We need time to build the true fans, establish the infrastructure, and create offers, products, and services that have been tested. When you have the connections, the collaborations, the trust, and the momentum like that race car cruising in that video game, then it's the time to hit the turbo button.

And if you do, it's stunning how easily you will shoot to victory, just like Bobby.

Make Not Fitting In a Career

"I thought not fitting in was something I had to fix. Now I see it as my superpower." — MAXIME LAGACÉ

Our son Andrew has been fascinated with bugs since he was four years old. When we asked him what he wanted for Christmas that year, he enthusiastically said he wanted a tarantula. When stated clearly that we were not bringing a tarantula into our home, we asked what else he would like.

"A scorpion," he countered.

We hoped it was just a fad. It wasn't. Over the next few years, the books he read, artwork he created, and things he studied revolved around bugs. He played sports, and did all of the things that "normal" kids do, but his thirst for learning about bugs was unquenchable. When he was six, he initiated a conversation about how humans couldn't survive without bugs. We amused him in the conversation until he stated enough facts to get us to understand how he was, in fact, correct.

When he was eleven, Andrew decided he wasn't interested in playing baseball that year. The neighbors and other parents were confused. One dad asked why he wouldn't play baseball. *Every* kid plays baseball. I waited to hear his response.

"I'm not concerned if everyone is playing it. I'm not interested. I'm really interested in learning more about bugs and teaching others about it," he responded.

The next week, we planted our chairs on the third base side of the field our son Nolan got set for his game. As I watched Nolan and his teammates do battle in their uniforms, I heard a commotion behind me. I turned to see that Andrew had caught a snake. One of the mothers screamed, but the kids around him were fascinated. Within a minute, there were a dozen kids surrounding him. They were asking all sorts of questions, and Andrew calmly answered all of them. It was then that some parents started approaching the circle, as curious as the kids. He began teaching them too.

I turned back to the field, then back to Andrew. In front of me there was a group of kids wearing the same thing, playing the same game, because that's what everyone does. Behind me was a kid who didn't follow everyone else. He followed his curiosity. He even got made fun of because of that. Yet, there he was, attracting his own crowd. Leading and teaching, like he always wanted. He told us for years that his goal was to show others who are afraid of spiders, scorpions, snakes, and insects that they are good for the environment and aren't as dangerous or scary as they have been made out to be.

Five years later, that passion never subsided. For years, Elizabeth and I attempted to convince Andrew to start a business around what he loved so much. But he is stubborn, like his dad. He didn't want to do it. One afternoon, we headed over to Clearwater Beach, and he brought one of his eight tarantulas with him. The response he got was off the charts. People asking questions, wanting to hold it, take pictures with it and—most importantly to him—learn. Without his asking, someone gave him a ten-dollar tip for being so helpful. I told him that I'd take him again the next day, but he needed to bring a tip cup so people could support him. He agreed. That afternoon, he brought home nearly fifty dollars.

On the drive home, I told him how great he did. He said the coolest part was seeing that he could make people who were scared of spiders get over their fears. He then looked down at the cup and the money in it. He couldn't believe he got $50 in tips for being out there for two hours.

"Did that feel like work?" I asked.

"Work?" he said.

"That's a business right there," I explained. "You provide value, and people show their appreciation by paying you for it. Did it feel like work?"

"Not at all. That was fun! I would do that every day!" he exclaimed.

The next few weeks, the beach was hopping during Spring Break. We went out together five days a week, for two weeks. He spent about five hours each day letting people hold the tarantula and the scorpion while answering questions. One woman, not knowing I was his dad, told me that she learned more that day than she did in all her science classes in school. The praise continued.

"I've been frightened by spiders my entire life," one muscular, heavily tattooed man told Andrew. "And you just helped me get over my greatest fear. Thank you for being here and doing this!"

After two weeks, he walked away with more than $1,600 in tips and countless people not fearing tarantulas and scorpions for the first time in their lives. The success convinced him to build a website, then a blog, a series of videos, and an e-book. The interest has led to him doing birthday parties for kids and events for companies and churches where he brings his bugs to educate, inform, and inspire.

But there was one moment that had a profound effect. Before the business started, we preached about building a network and being generous with people. Early in his studies, he came across a man named Steve Kutcher on YouTube. Kutcher is also a bug lover. He creates amazing pieces of art with the bugs. He is the guy Hollywood calls when they need spiders and scorpions in the movies. In *Spiderman*, *The Scorpion King*, and *Arachnophobia*, Kutcher was the man behind the bugs in those movies.

Instead of reaching out and asking for anything, we did a homeschool lesson where Andrew wrote a letter thanking him for his work and asking questions. Elizabeth and I went to bed concerned that Kutcher wouldn't respond and Andrew would get discouraged. We both woke up like kids on Christmas morning when we saw his response in our email. They quickly established a friendship, and when we visited California, Kutcher invited him to an event as a guest, then gave him a bug net and other gifts. On our next trip out, he invited Andrew and me to his home and a tour of his collection.

As we were leaving, we thanked him again for everything he had done to encourage and inspire Andrew. His words back were special but also a warning for many.

"I knew from the first letter that Andrew was a giver," Kutcher stated. "He reached out and complimented me and didn't ask for anything. I get a lot of people that reach out to me. There are a lot of takers out there. So when I find a giver, I want to do anything I can to help them."

I'd be an awful father if I didn't give him a shameless plug. You can check out Andrew's website at bugzrule.com and find him on Instagram @bugzrule88.

When You Think About Quitting

"Don't quit. You're already in pain. You're already hurt. Get a reward from it."

— ERIC THOMAS

I sat in my car waiting to get a haircut, having no clue that it wouldn't take place for a few more hours. I awaited a phone call from John VanDerMeulen, a friend and a member of our mastermind. The usually mild-mannered VanDerMeulen was unusually frustrated.

His business selling bird feeders on Amazon was stagnant. The hoops he had to jump through with Amazon, the struggle in growing their ranking, and the time it took to go essentially nowhere had him wanting to chuck it all. Quit the business. Quit the Mastermind. Quit it all.

I was going to do everything I could to not let him. He has a way of thinking, and a process of working, where I never doubted his eventual success. The way he can analyze products and research the details of it and have patience to allow it to come together were uncommon skills in my eyes.

But the results weren't there, and he had reached his breaking point. The conversation was the most tense and confrontational we'd ever had. In fact, we had never had anything close to a tense call since I met him a few years earlier. But here I was being the pest that I can be, challenging him in ways he didn't want to be challenged.

It was obvious in his voice that he wasn't the John who showed up every week on our calls. If he was going to quit the mastermind, I felt like I had failed him because we didn't do what we needed to do for him. For him to go out like that would be a sad ending to a great run together.

"So you are just going to quit?" I said to him sharply.

"I don't know what else to do," he snapped back.

That led to a flurry of questions about what he could do to keep it going, what wasn't being done and what the future could look like if he consistently did those things.

Somehow he decided not to quit. He accepted my challenge to message me every day with what he did and the progress he made. Good, bad, or indifferent, he needed to do that every day. I told him that I wouldn't respond to all of the messages. I didn't want a back and forth where he could question himself. We just needed to develop a habit and momentum.

He accepted. For the next few months, he messaged me every single day. What he didn't do was quit. Months later, he continued the accountability with Ken Carfagno, who needed the back and forth like John did.

Two years ago, ready to quit all of it, John VanDerMeulen made a decision to bet on himself. Every day he was going to do something to progress his business. And every day, he did.

While I was writing this book- on his birthday- he finalized a deal where he sold the business to a group of investors for nearly a half million dollars. That immediately got us to coin a nickname for him: John VanDerMillion. It might be my favorite story to come out of *Total Life Freedom* since we started because of what he struggled with, the work he put in, and the results it created.

It's easy to quit. The timing isn't right. The market isn't there. There is too much uncertainty. It's hard to keep going when you've lost hope. To get up the next day when you aren't feeling it and to still do the work. To put a smile on your face and work when you have little confidence in yourself and even less in your business. Everyone struggling wants to know how to turn things around quickly. What they ought to ask is "What can I do today and every day going forward to slowly get better?" Quick fixes lead to desperate decisions. Consistent action leads to long-term success. When I challenged John, I had no thoughts of him selling the business. I just wanted him to make a profitable endeavor for his family.

For him to do that, and to do it so well, set him and his family up for the next level of their lives. It's something that inspired all of us in the mastermind community. So, if you are on the verge of quitting—if you think there is nothing there and are yelling into the abyss—remember John VanDerMeulen. Reread this story. Find someone to hold you accountable. Find someone who believes in you enough not to let you quit.

You too might get the word *million* attached to the end of your name.

Create Wisely

"Happiness comes from giving, not getting. If we try hard to bring happiness to others, we cannot stop it from coming to us also. To get joy, we must give it, and to keep joy, we must scatter it." — JOHN TEMPLETON

Courtney Wisely grew up dirt poor. It's not surprising that she didn't have a healthy family environment around her. In 2007, she also didn't have a home. Wisely was not only living out of her car, she was also very pregnant. While she didn't have any money, she did possess a heart for others. She also has a mind that can figure out automation the way most of us can only dream of.

For the past few years, Courtney used those skills to help other cleaning business owners automate their services. These entrepreneurs worked like artists but couldn't think like a businessperson. They trudged through the work and made their money. It was incredibly inefficient, but they truly didn't know another way. Their customers raved about them, and their work was of the highest quality, but they always seemed like a dog chasing its own tail.

And then they were introduced to Courtney, who proceeded to rock their world. With the same ease that the cleaner vacuumed the floor in record time with a perfect pattern, Courtney went through their mess of information and laid out a plan of automation so they could focus on what they did best. She astonished them with how well and how fast that she set this up.

But because of her upbringing, she had little understanding of money and had relatively no self-worth when it came to finances. She failed to see the value in what she offered, so Courtney wound up doing all of this work for free. I'm not talking about twenty minutes here and there type of work. I'm talking about flying to a different city and spending four days revolutionizing these people's businesses during multiple-day retreats. When we first met in October of 2019, she described her process. My mouth dropped open.

"You are doing all of this—changing these people's lives—and what are you charging?" I asked.

"Well," she said, embarrassed, "they go ahead and pay for my room at the retreat."

I couldn't believe what I was hearing. I asked how long she had done this. My jaw dropped further when she mentioned that she's been doing those free retreats for two years. I was dumbfounded. She was obviously struggling with money, so I asked why she wasn't charging for her work.

Her response was slow and apologetic.

"I don't…know," she dragged out with an uncomfortable laugh. "I don't know how to charge for things. Anyway, I absolutely love doing it. I don't need to get paid. I'm not good with money. I just love helping them turn their businesses around!"

I am not going to dive into her mindset on money and sense of self-worth at this moment. I think we can all see the issues she faced. What I do want to focus on is her heart.

Despite her money mindset issues—and possibly because of them—she was able to do something most people won't do. She built a raving fan base and honed a skill set that had the biggest names in her industry taking notice. Courtney did what I preach to the 100x level. She connected and created so generously that she built up an army of support. She gave without expectation relentlessly.

Now hear me when I say that I am not asking you to build your business this way. I'm simply pointing out what happened when Courtney did.

When we connected, she had people knocking down her door for her help. She dug the riverbed so deep and so strong that when the water was added, it flowed mightily. She joined the *Total Life Freedom Mastermind* shortly after. And after some tough love, she got over her fear of charging. For the new people asking about her service, Courtney offered the retreat for $975. She sold out ten spots almost immediately.

We pushed her to raise it again. At $1,500, it sold out just as fast.

Same thing at $2,000 per person.

In the spring, five months later, she was getting $3,000 per person at these retreats, and everyone was thrilled to pay it.

And then Covid-19 hit. Live events crumbled. She came back to us distraught. As fast as the business was built, it was all gone.

"Why can't you take this online?" Jerad Spencer, a member of the mastermind, asked.

"It's not possible," she responded. "I can't do this work online for them. It needs to be in person!"

Two weeks later, though, she turned the information she had into an online boot camp. Less than six months later, that online boot camp had earned her more than $100,000 with the potential for unlimited growth. Not only that, but she had unexpectedly built a location-independent business that only required her time a few hours a week.

As incredible as her story is, I don't want the money to be the focus here. Because none of those financial successes would have happened without what she did before it started rolling in. She focused on solving others' problems. She didn't worry about her business plan. She didn't even set selfish goals. Even though she was insecure about herself, Courtney's goal was to help others achieve their goals.

What happened? She built a following like no other. By doing it for free, she opened the door to let people in, but she didn't just help others. She helped herself. By doing all of those retreats, she got better fast. She honed her skills much quicker than if she were charging because she had many more people to work with. When she made mistakes, they were early, and they were free. Her speed of development was faster and more effective simply because she took on so many with so little pressure. And those people told their friends and their business associates.

Before she knew it (which might have been late in the game!) people were beating down her door. They couldn't get to her because the line was so long. So when she put the price tag up, people were clambering to get to the front of the line. And in 2021, she made more money than she did every prior year of her life—combined!

The Well Connected Beginner

"It's better to start as a fool and learn from your mistakes than to fake being a genius and ignore your errors." —JAMES CLEAR

Jordan Harbinger was the host of one of the most successful podcasts in the world. He was the host for more than a decade while helping build the show toward a whopping four million downloads per month. With all of that success, he found himself unceremoniously fired from his position.

Even though the show was built with a team, Jordan was the host, the head of sales and the one who brought in the leads. That podcast was focused on dating. But after Jordan got married, his interest shifted away from the topic of the show. Unfortunately, his business partners didn't have the same vision. It led to negativity, disagreements, and then eventually an "amicable split." The split didn't go as it was supposed to go. Major legal issues continued until the split became less than amicable.

After nearly twelve years hosting the show, Jordan found himself out of that business altogether. It was then that he had no choice but to start over. He describes sleepless nights worrying about the legal issues, the uncertainty, and the struggle to begin again. He decided to create *The Jordan Harbinger Show* using the content he envisioned when he was a part of the previous show.

At the end of his time at that show, he described an environment that felt toxic to his team, many of whom only stayed because of him. So when he was fired, he didn't leave alone. Because of those strong relationships, the members of his team followed him to his new show.

"When you find yourself on the outside of anything, you find yourself with either your talent and skills, or your talent, skills, and your network," Jordan said. "*If* you have a network. I'm always creating and maintaining relationships. It's just the way I like to live."

After maintaining those relationships for more than eleven years—consistently being generous, helpful, and giving without expectation—he found himself in a dire spot. And having rarely asked for anything, he needed help. So he reached out to hundreds of friends and asked for support. Without an email list, website, Twitter account, or Facebook page—all Jordan had was his network.

When it all crumbled, Jordan was told that he'd find out who his true friends were. And that wasn't said in a good way. Meaning many people you thought were your friends will abandon you. He found some of that, but he also found the opposite. When they heard his story, friends and listeners volunteered to help. He had people introducing him to people who could help him.

People like Pat Flynn, from *Smart Passive Income*, emailed his entire list about Jordan's new podcast and offered him another spot on his top-ranked podcast. Jordan had quality writers step up to write blog posts, show notes, and worksheets for the podcast. He had professional firms reach out to work on search engine optimization for his website. And they all did it on a volunteer basis to give to Jordan after all he had given to them.

And as it all started, he had a generous, wealthy member of his podcast network— Norm Pattis—go out of his way to get him over the hump. He cut him a check so money wouldn't be a worry. It was an advance on his new show so Jordan didn't miss an episode. And then, Norm filed a lawsuit against his former partners so they would be so busy dealing with him that they wouldn't have time for Jordan.

We often hear about people that come out of the woodwork because they now *want something*. Jordan built such a wealth of connection that he had people coming out of the woodwork *to help*.

"The only way to create something that is unique is to either outwork everyone, be more talented than everyone, or have better connections than everyone," Jordan said "And there is no way you should ever wait to create—and maintain—a relationship."

The Value of Creation

"I hate writing. I love having written." — DOROTHY PARKER

Creating is hard. It's lonely. It's painful. At times, it can seem as if nobody cares. You have learned that if you build it, they won't just come. You understand that you might fail, but at least you are going to fail at something cool. It's all bonus anyway, remember?

Maybe you have questioned why anyone would need what you have to offer. But, unlike everyone who quits, you don't. You have experienced playing to an empty room- either on stage or online. By doing so, you have been able to focus on the passionate few and begin creating a few true fans. You have done your best to avoid the curse of knowledge and become aware of that special thing that you have that may have been overlooked.

You may have created yourself a micro niche, which millions of others are doing as well. You've seen now that by having character and curiosity, you can connect and collaborate with like-minded people. You also get to be a conduit for those who need to hear your message. You are playing the long game, creating a content waterfall to reach more people effectively. You've become a magnet, attracting those who are for your work while repelling those who aren't.

And you aren't letting this success go to your head, right? Don't forget to laugh at yourself, and don't pretend to be someone who you aren't. You have seen that through pressure and time, you have created your own unique blend. You actually now have so many ideas that you create a future list. And when it's all put together, you will be ready to push the turbo button for exponential growth.

All while knowing that we're always starting over. No matter how much success we attain, we always- always- want to be a beginner.

CONCLUSION

"You spend the first half of your life breaking things and the second half of your life working to fix them." — JAMES HETFIELD

Both relationally and professionally, I did everything wrong before learning how to do it right. *But bad choices make great stories.* And great stories teach valuable lessons to help others. Professionally, this book will allow you to not only build real relationships and connections but also create a career in the area that you want and allow you to do everything better in business.

The Wealth of Connection comes before marketing. It comes before branding. It should be the foundation before thinking about lead generation, your pitch, and your strategies. You might also find that you don't need a lot of these things if you do this exceptionally well. Then, and only then, will you be ready to hit the turbo button. *The Wealth of Connection* allows anyone the option to change industries, add new offers, and be entirely flexible in their career pursuits—whether they are an entrepreneur or an employee.

It's vital to put your generous goals ahead of your selfish goals.

It's widely discussed that 70% of all jobs are not published, and the U.S. Bureau of Labor and Statistics concluded that 85% of all jobs are filled through personal connections and personal networks. According to LinkedIn's internal data, people who are referred for a job are nine times more likely to get it. Those are astounding numbers considering how undervalued and underestimated building a powerful network is seen.

The wealth is in the connection.

We send our kids to university to gain knowledge, yet in the end, we know that it is the network and connections that were built there that have true value. We join online communities to learn a skill or acquire information, and the adage about online communities rings true: they come for the content, but they stay for the community. We go to conferences to listen to a variety of speakers, but the wise ones know that the true value is in the hallways where valuable connections are made.

Of all of the skills to develop, there will be none more important than your people skills. How we communicate matters. How we respond to feedback matters. How we keep in touch with people in our network matters. How we show gratitude matters. All of the things we discussed in this book matter.

Culturally, we fawn over those who are a wealth of information. We showcase those who are a wealth of knowledge. We admire those who have a wealth of assets.

But those who are the most valuable to society are the ones who are a wealth of connection.

If You'd Like More

We can't end here! Even though *The Wealth of Connection* is done, there is still so much more to share. That's why I've created a weekly blog titled "The Connection." Every Monday, we will start the week with stories, lessons and insights on how to further build your wealth of connection with ideas that expand from this book. You can find The Connection at totallifefreedom.com.

Also, I am thrilled to announce my new podcast, *The Wealth of Connection,* will launch early this summer! *The Wealth of Connection Podcast* will feature conversations with some of the most connected and interesting people around as we dive deep into their mindset, work, and life. You can find it, along with *Total Life Freedom*, my daily, short form podcast, on any of your favorite podcast players or at totallifefreedom.com.

My Ask To You

Thank you for reading *The Wealth of Connection*. The biggest help that you could do would be to share this book with someone that you think could benefit from it. If you know someone who can't afford it, email me at vincent@totallifefreedom.com and I will gift them a digital copy. If you would be interested in leaving an honest review on Amazon, that is one of the greatest ways you can help. It allows others to find the book easier and spread this message!

About The Author

Vincent Pugliese is, most importantly, a husband to his wife, Elizabeth, and father to their three sons, Andrew, Nolan and Dylan. Vincent and his family live in Bradenton, Florida, where they homeschool their children through interest-based learning.

Vincent is keynote speaker, the host of the Total Life Freedom Podcast, the author of Freelance to Freedom, and the owner of The Total Life Freedom Mastermind Community for entrepreneurs and those looking to become entrepreneurs to build a life of time, money and location freedom.

Website- totallifefreedom.com

Podcasts- Total Life Freedom and The Wealth of Connection

Community- totallifefreedom.com

Instagram- totallifefreedom1

Email- vincent@totallifefreedom.com

Acknowledgements

To start, it would be impossible to name all of the people who have helped contribute to this book. A second book would be required for that. Everything you have just read is because of the amazing people that have come into my life. If I know you, your actions, words, and your life have contributed in some way to *The Wealth of Connection*. This doesn't take into account the thousands upon thousands of people who have produced, created, and published work that has influenced the content in this book. I hope each of you is feeling the psychic compensation coming your way.

First and foremost, thank you to Elizabeth Pugliese. Your endless support of all of my crazy dreams and visions is what makes all of this possible. Thank you for putting up with my incessant ramblings about this book for the past three years, for being patient as I repeated thoughts and maintaining your loving spirit and support throughout all of this. You are the best and I love you with all of my heart!

Nolan: Your creativity has no limits. You amaze me with your boundless interests. It's a joy to watch you as you become the helpful, generous, and loving young man that you are. Your hugs are the absolute best, and your smile is unforgettable. Your sense of adventure was perfectly displayed this morning as you fished during a big storm!

Andrew: It is a joy to watch you inspire so many with your passions to teach others about bugs and help them get over their fears. Your giving spirit and willingness to always be a help- either to strangers, at church, or at home (well, maybe not there) :), makes me a proud dad.

Dylan: As you read this, I would bet that you are either taking apart some form of electronics or building something from discarded electronics. It's just a hunch. Your endless energy, creativity, and passion are inspiring. There is no better way for me to end the night than by either reading you a book or telling you a story. That won't last, so I treasure each one.

To my parents, Vinny and Carleen. Each year that passes, I appreciate more and more what you have done for me. I will be the first to say that I didn't always understand or appreciate it. Yet the life that I have is due to your love, guidance, and your allowing "me to be me." Aside from what you have given me, your marriage of more than five decades has given our family a rock-solid foundation on which to build. I couldn't be more grateful.

Steve- The role of the "Fun Uncle" could not have been played by anyone better than you. Your love of our family is so appreciated, and our conversations only get better. The boys absolutely adore you and all that you bring to their lives. And you need to pass along the "gift giving" genes because you took them all- your gifting is so unique and creative, and I'm just terrible at it!

To Kent Sanders: thanks for your guidance, coaching, and patience in helping create this book. John Briggs- Thank you for your detailed editing of *The Wealth of Connection*. Jennifer Harshman: Thank you for your editing magic to improve many areas of this book. Anthony Casto: thank you for all of your hard work, creativity, and collaboration in creating this book cover and all of the inner pages. Courtney Wisely: thanks a million for being our chaos coordinator! And Paul Cuneo: thank you for bringing things out of my work that I would never have seen without you.

To all of my friends and members of *The Total Life Freedom Mastermind Community*- both present and past- it's an honor to go through life together with you. Your generosity, connection, and friendships prove to me that you can love the work that you do, make friends within it, and develop a life of your dreams all at the same time. I give thanks to each and every one of you.

This is always the hardest part- naming names. I cringe thinking about leaving someone out. Scott Beynon, in the short time that our family knew you, you made an everlasting impact. Bruce Baumann, thank you for taking a chance on Elizabeth and me and for teaching such wonderful life lessons. Ken Carfagno and the Carfagno family, thanks for your wonderful friendship. My life changed for the better the day I met you. Dan Miller, this book wouldn't be a thing without your mentorship. For all of the names below, and so many not written, I wish I could write so much more.

But thank you for those of you who inspired stories and quotes within *The Wealth of Connection*: Funzi, Chris Tuff, Bob Beaudine, Seth Godin, Don Wettrick, Chad Jeffers, Jim Dooley, Mike Snyder, John Ruhlin, John Stange, Fred Klein, Joe Elbert, James Malinchak, Gustavo Fernandez, Mark Fujiwara, Jonathan Mendonza, Brad Barrett, Chuck Bennett, Michael O'Neal, Bob Beaudine, Larry Hagner, Andy Andrews, Joe Saul-Sehy, Nick Elkins, Carolyn Gundersen, John VanDerMeulen, Tim Ferriss, Jared Easley, Donald Kelly, Chuck Bennett, Ed Betz, Jordan Harbinger, Donna Stapleton, John Lee Dumas, Kate Erickson, Joanne Miller, Ben Killoy, Michael Nania, Bob Hubbard, Brant Christopher Menswar, Chris Niemeyer, Josh Brown, Roger Whitney, Nick Pavlidis, Devon Bandison, Jerad Spencer, Steve Kutcher, and many, many more!

Many stories worthy of printing didn't make the book. There was one that changed my life and career in one night. Jim Jorden, thank you so much.

Thank you to all of the podcasters who have had me as a guest on your show to help spread the word. Those conversations are a highlight for me. I wish I could name you all.

To Pastor Steve Coad and all of the members of Oasis Church in Bradenton, Florida. Thank you for welcoming our family into your family. It's a pleasure to have our family a part of such an amazing, generous community.

Although it might not appear that way, this book is one of the most challenging projects I have ever undertaken. It has gone through a half dozen name changes, countless rewritings and stories that haven't made these pages. I wrote the words on these pages- this wasn't an outsourced project. This is my heart and soul. It's kept me up all night and has given me too many moments of doubt to count.

It's made me wonder if I'm a hypocrite and if I'm even the one to write this book.

But it's done something that each book should do to its author. It's made me a better person. More often than you would know, this project has made me ask myself, "Are you that person that you are writing about, or is it the person that you are writing for?" Every day, every hour, this project forces me to become a better person than I am at that moment. And although I hope this book improves so many lives for the better, I know with 100% certainty that all of this work is going to make at least one person better in each area written in this book: me.

To conclude, I want to thank you for reading *The Wealth of Connection*. There are unlimited options that you can choose to do with your time and I'm honored that you took your time to read this book. I hope it's been valuable to you and will improve your life and the lives around you. I couldn't ask for more than that.

The Wealth of Connectors

I am honoring the people that went out of their way to help, provide feedback, and support the creation and launch of *The Wealth of Connection.*

M.J. James	Dan Hinz	Ciara Carter
Cleve Page	David Steininger	Chris Comer
Michael Grant	Lukas Loveland	Phil Pavely
Jodi Krangle	Marcus Rangel	James Cermak
Michael Boly	Greg Gerber	David Cook
Nathan Boyd	Heidi Hood	Katlynn Pyatt

Adam Zach	Teresa McCloy	Brad Coleman
Debra Ekhert	Marianne Renner	Ian Barford
Ben Killoy	Georgui Kasaev	Cole James
Aaron Hunt	Jake Van Ness	Doc Green
Marcus Gates	Chris Knighton	Christina Kines
J.D. Elliott	Armando Garcia	John Stange
Javier Mesa	Troy Stoneking	Parker Nash
Ken Carfagno	John Kenny	Mike Snyder
Colin Chambers	Elaine Grant	Vickie Smith
Mark Coomer	Ken Hannaman	Greg Tosi
Cliff Feightner	Fred Marshall	Barry Karch
Bill Brent	Patrick Conlon	Jason Bahr
Ian Roth	Angie Garcia	Tony Slabaugh
Mark Ross	Leisa Peterson	Philipp Lomboy
Michael Jones	Jason Krivickas	Dee Gaudette
Melinda Edwards	Chris Schwab	Lindsay Reiling
Renee Vidor	Miriam Santiago	Scott Johnson
Melinda Walker	Emily Brunner	Justin Hertz
Jody Pistore	Karen Griffard Putz	Rick Blodgett
Jeff McMahon	Chris Saturnio	Paul Grivas
Jeremy Stiehl	Tyler Greathouse	Jure Mandic
Diana Bader	Patty Griffiths Perkins	Jeff Bogaczyk
Kyle Martin	Robert Bradley Miller	Cathy Yost
Glasa Gottschalk	Kathy Dufour	Rich Avery
Kathy De La Torre	Raejan Noh	Brad Ritter
John VanDerMeulen	Ryan Olsen	Kenny Carfagno
John Russell	Kristen Ricupero	Chad Gordon
R.L. Shawver	Ashley Taylor	Armando Cruz
Craig Ambrosio	Dee Ann Piercy Schnautz	

Printed in Great Britain
by Amazon

23519118R00138